ANTHROPOLOGICAL PAPERS

MUSEUM OF ANTHROPOLOGY, UNIVERSITY OF MICHIGAN
NO. 37

OBSIDIAN ANALYSES AND PREHISTORIC NEAR EASTERN TRADE: 7500 TO 3500 B.C.

BY
GARY A. WRIGHT

ANN ARBOR
THE UNIVERSITY OF MICHIGAN, 1969

© 1969 by the Regents of the University of Michigan
The Museum of Anthropology
All rights reserved

ISBN (print): 978-1-949098-11-2
ISBN (ebook): 978-1-951519-33-9

Browse all of our books at
sites.lsa.umich.edu/archaeology-books.

Order our books from the University of Michigan
Press at www.press.umich.edu.

For permissions, questions, or manuscript queries,
contact Museum publications by email at umma-pubs@umich.edu or visit the Museum website at
lsa.umich.edu/ummaa.

FOREWORD

THIS WORK is a rewriting and reediting of my doctoral dissertation which was submitted to the University of Michigan in June, 1968. I wish to thank the members of my doctoral committee, Professors Robert Whallon, Jr. (chairman), Richard Beardsley, William Farrand, Adon A. Gordus, James B. Griffin, and Jeffrey Parsons, for their helpful comments and suggestions during the preparation of the dissertation.

The obsidian studies were initiated at the University of Michigan under the co-direction of J. B. Griffin, of the Museum of Anthropology and Dr. A. A. Gordus, of the Department of Chemistry, and followed the lead of Cann and Renfrew's (1964) work on Mediterranean obsidians. I should like to thank Drs. Robert J. Braidwood, Halet Çambel, J. R. Cann, Jean Perrot, Colin Renfrew, and Henry T. Wright for the Near Eastern obsidian specimens reported on here. Braidwood and Perrot also provided data on sites which they are currently excavating but which have not been fully published. A major part of the support for the analysis of the obsidian came from the National Science Foundation Grant, No. G. S. —1196 to Griffin and Gordus. The analytical work was done by Gordus and his associates.

Dr. K. V. Flannery was originally scheduled to be a member of the doctoral committee, however field work commitments prevented him from attending the defense. Dr. Flannery kindly read most of what is published here and provided me with a number of helpful suggestions and ideas, as well as unpublished data. Dr. Frank Hole allowed me to utilize the unpublished data from his doctoral dissertation on Jarmo and Sarab (Hole, n.d.).

My early interest in the problems of Near Eastern prehistory was stimulated and encouraged by one of my former teachers, Dr. Arthur J. Jelinek. Drs. Jelinek and Braidwood and Mrs. Linda Braidwood first introduced me to fieldwork in the Near East.

I wish also to thank Dr. Richard A. Watson, Washington University, St. Louis, who accompanied me on a survey of obsidian sources in Central and Eastern Turkey during October and November, 1968. Unhappily, adverse conditions prevented us from collecting from many obsidian flows.

FOREWORD

All of the above deserve my thanks. None of them, however, should be held responsible for my interpretations of the elemental, geological, ethnological, or archaeological data.

January 5, 1969
Gary A. Wright
Cleveland, Ohio

CONTENTS

I.	The Problem	1
II.	Obsidian Sources in the Near East	5
III.	Obsidian in the Near East: 7500 to 3500 B.C.	17
	Distribution	17
	Uses	27
	Trade and Transport	45
IV.	Near Eastern Trade: 7500 to 3500 B.C.	53
	Sources of Other Raw Materials	54
	The Preceramic: 7500 to 6250 B.C.	57
	The Early Ceramic Phases: 6250 to 5200 B.C.	62
	Halaf—Ubaid	67
V.	Conclusions	77
	References	85

I

THE PROBLEM

THE STUDY of trade in prehistoric times has been of some interest to archaeologists for a considerable period of time. The recovery of exotic, nonlocal raw materials and/or craft items in an excavation poses a number of interrelated questions. When Squier and Davis first unearthed obsidian artifacts in Hopewellian mounds in the eastern United States 120 years ago, they were aware of these problems. They commented: "To measure the bounds of intercourse, casual or constant, or define the course of migration, it is necessary to ascertain the exact primitive locality of the product in question" (Squier and Davis, 1848: 278).

First of all, then, we are interested in what source or sources were being utilized. When this question is answered, the archaeologist is in a position to accept, to reformulate or to reject the hypotheses about the nature of the trade system with which he has been working.

We may take the Hopewellian obsidian a step further. More than 10,000 pieces of obsidian, ranging from chipping debris and cores to well-made ceremonial objects have been recovered in Hopewellian sites in the Scioto Valley, Ohio. Guesses as to the source area from which this raw material was derived have included Alaska, the Pacific Coast of North America, Yellowstone National Park, the southwestern United States, and central Mexico. In no case have there been any petrological or chemical (elemental composition) data offered in support. Although some data on the elemental composition of different obsidian flows in Yellowstone Park have been available since 1899 (Iddings, 1899), no systematic examination of Hopewellian obsidian in reference to its composition was undertaken until 1966. To anticipate some of the results to be presented elsewhere, neutron activation analysis studies at the University of Michigan have clearly demonstrated that the Hopewellian obsidian derived from two separate flows in Yellowstone Park (Griffin *et al.*, 1969).

In the particular case of the Hopewell, the source of the obsidian has anthropological implications. For example, a number of investigators have seen similarities between cultural traits in various areas of Mexico (never as one complex) and in Hopewell. Among these is the presence of obsidian. If the Hopewellian obsidian had been shown to have derived from a source in Mexico, the hypothesis of contact between the two regions would have found some measure of support.

In some cases, there is little problem in determining the origin of a particular nonlocal object. For example, certain marine shell species may occur only in restricted ecological habitats. Once identified as to species by a specialist, their sources may be easily located. In other cases, more sophisticated techniques must be employed. There were five source areas, each with a large number of separate obsidian flows, which had to be examined before the sources of Hopewellian obsidian could be unambiguously identified.

Obsidian is a raw material that was widely used and traded in most major areas of the world. For this reason alone it is worthy of inquiry. The hypothesis that each obsidian flow has a characteristic element composition of its own has been examined elsewhere (Gordus *et al.*, 1968; Wright, n.d.). No two obsidian flows will have exactly the same chemical composition.[1] This being the case, obsidian artifacts may be related not only to a source area but to a particular flow.

Using these data gained from chemical analysis as a background, the second problem is the determination of patterns in the use and trade of this particular raw material in the Near East between 7500 and 3500 B.C. There are a number of factors to consider in this type of analysis. (1) There are two major source areas in the Near East, each containing a number of flows: Central Anatolia and the Lake Van region of Eastern Anatolia. What is the changing pattern of utilization and distribution of obsidian from each source area and each flow during the time period under consideration? What does this tell us about contacts between different areas at particular points in time? (2) Artifacts of the same raw material may function differently in different social and economic contexts. What is the nature of the usage of obsidian in different areas, or on different sites within the same area, at a particular point in time; and how does the utilization of the product change through time within the context of a single evolving cultural system? In short, we need to know the uses to which a raw material was put, and the economic and social contexts in which it occurs. (3) How much of the raw material is present? Is it only a few

---

[1] Our studies indicate quite clearly that "appearance characteristics" (e.g. color, etc.) are not valid criteria for distinguishing obsidian flows unambiguously (see Frison *et al.*, 1968; Renfrew *et al.*, 1965; Wright, n.d.: Chapter II).

blades or does it constitute a major proportion of the assemblage? A quantitative study of the material may assist in showing whether or not a regular system of exchange was being maintained.

Trade operates within economic, social, and ideological spheres of culture. The form which an exchange system assumes is dependent upon and conditioned by the social and economic complexities of the groups involved. That is, the mechanics of exchange between bands is not the same as between states.

There are a number of points which the archaeologist must consider. (1) Beyond the band level, there are generally two kinds of trade; local and long distance trade as they are termed by Harding (1967). The first generally deals with foodstuffs between kinsmen or near kinsmen. The second is often concerned primarily with raw materials. It is this kind of trade which archaeologists usually consider. For example, it is this type of trade with which Çlark (1952: 241-81) is dealing. In many cases, however, long distance trade is of far less economic importance to the group than the local trade. (2) At the tribal and band levels, trade goods are generally not accumulated by individuals, but are redistributed. This is particularly true with the foodstuffs, but occasionally less true of long distance trade goods which may serve as status symbols.[2] Above these cultural levels, goods like craft items are usually accumulated and very seldom redistributed. They often serve as symbols of status differentiation for the higher ranking members of lineages (Flannery, 1968b). (3) The plotting of trade goods on a distribution map is only part of the solution to the problem. It is necessary to know the local ecological situation and subsistence economics so that nonperishable goods may also be considered, to have some idea of the local social organization so that the trade mechanics may be discussed, and to utilize data on how trade goods are employed so that the relationship between the exchange system and local status and ceremony may be clarified.

Finally, we will consider the changing patterns of trade in the Near East, both local and long distance, between 7500 and 3500 B.C. This time period begins with the origin of settled farming villages and ends with the final stages prior to the origin of the state in alluvial southern Mesopotamia. It also coincides with the major utilization of obsidian.

The data are extremely poor for many of the necessary facets needed for a useful discussion of prehistoric trade. For example,

---

[2] See, for example, Winter's (1968) stimulating paper on long distance trade during the Late Archaic in the southeastern United States, and the utilization of trade goods as grave furniture.

for many cultural phases there are no subsistence data available. For many sites there are absolutely no counts available for any artifacts. For many raw materials, there are either a number of sources which might have been exploited, or there are no known sources. In some cases, the source of a product is vaguely assigned to a region, like "Iran." This should indicate how badly the obsidian studies need to be extended to other raw materials such as copper, iron oxides, flint, marble, etc.

Thus, in this last section I claim to have solved no problem. I have attempted, however, to raise a number of important questions and to outline where the necessary data for answering these questions are lacking. Rather than solving problems, I have presented a series of hypotheses or models to explain the changing pattern of trade in certain subareas of the Near East. Almost all of the relevant data still must be collected in order to test these hypotheses. As Hole and Flannery (1968: 204) phrased it: ". . . we can pose hypotheses which, like all hypotheses, are fair game for attack and subsequent refinement; but hopefully, when refined, they will add a useful new dimension to our explanations."

II

OBSIDIAN SOURCES IN THE NEAR EAST

IN TERMS of the amount of integrated work on both source and site specimens, there are more data currently available on the percentages of different chemical elements present in Near Eastern obsidians than for obsidian from any other area. (For the average percentages of the different elements present in obsidian and for the abbreviations used to refer to these elements, see Table 1.) At present, we may distinguish two major geographical foci of obsidian sources in this area. One of these is in Central Anatolia and the other is centered in the Lake Van region of eastern Turkey. There are no known sources in western Turkey, Iran, Iraq, or the Levant.

Seven obsidian localities (Map 1) have been investigated in the Aksary-Nevşehir-Niğde region of central Turkey (Wright *et al.*, in

TABLE 1

COMPOSITION OF AN AVERAGE OBSIDIAN SAMPLE

Element		Per Cent Content	Element		Per Cent Content
O	(Oxygen)	42	C	(Carbon)	0.01
Si	(Silicon)	40	La	(Lanthanum)	0.01
Al	(Aluminum)	7	Nb	(Niobium)	0.005
K	(Potassium)	3.4	Li	(Lithium)	0.004
Na	(Sodium)	3.0	Y	(Yttrium)	0.004
Fe	(Iron)	2.2	Sb	(Antimony)	0.003
Ca	(Calcium)	0.8	Cs	(Cesium)	0.003
Ti	(Titanium)	0.2	Yb	(Ytterbium)	0.003
H	(Hydrogen)	0.2	Pb	(Lead)	0.002
P	(Phosphorus)	0.06	Ga	(Gallium)	0.002
Zn	(Zinc)	0.05	Hf	(Hafnium)	0.001
Ba	(Barium)	0.05	V	(Vanadium)	0.001
Co	(Cobalt)	0.03	Sm	(Samarium)	0.0005
Mn	(Manganese)	0.02	Mo	(Molybdenum)	0.0004
Rb	(Rubidium)	0.02	Sc	(Scandium)	0.0002
Mg	(Magnesium)	0.02	Lu	(Luteium)	0.0001
Sr	(Strontium)	0.01	Ir	(Iridium)	0.000004
Zr	(Zirconium)	0.01			

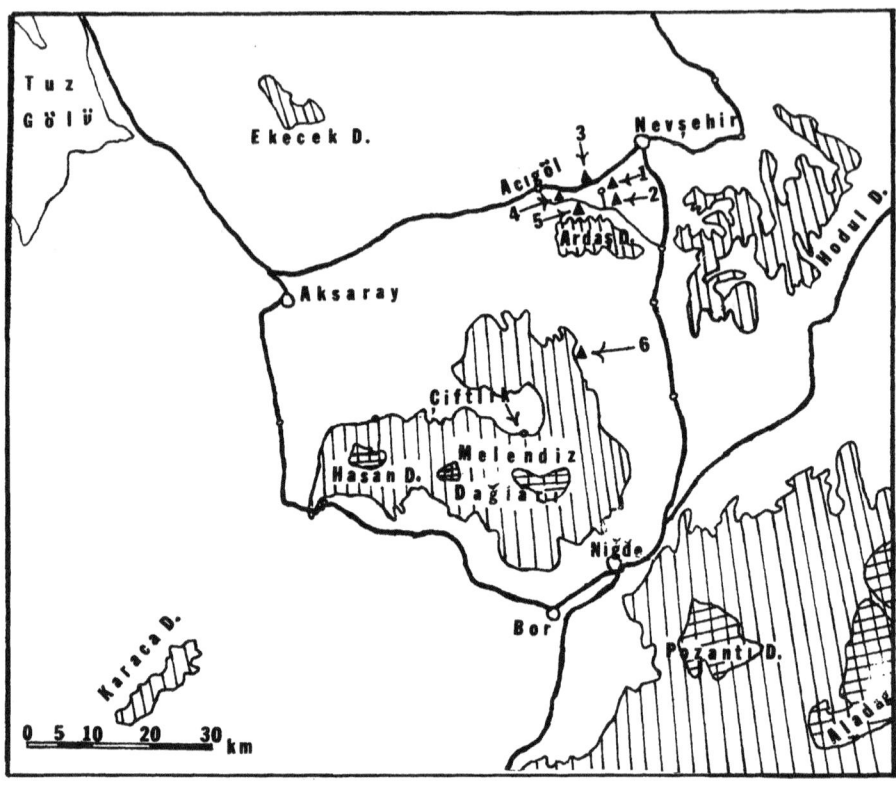

Map 1. Obsidian localities in the Nevşehir-Aksaray-Niğde region, Central Anatolia.

press). Five of these stations are located east of the village of Acigöl, which lies about 16 km. west of Nevşehir. Locality 6 crops out on the east slope of the Korkuyu ridge which belongs to the Göllü Dağ mass. This locality is about 30 km. south of Acigöl. The village of Çiftlik is located about 40 km. northwest of Niğde and 42 km. southwest of Acigöl. The geology of these obsidian flows is discussed more extensively elsewhere (Wright et al., in press).

Localities 2 and 3 are termed the Acigöl-Topada source by Renfrew, Dixon and Cann (1966), and is their obsidian group 1e-f.[1]

---

[1] An obsidian group refers to a series of samples which exhibit similar elemental contents. The groups were originally defined by Renfrew and his associates. The more neutral term "group" is used rather than source because some sources have not yet been located.

The Çiftlik source is their group 2b. Element data are also available for Localities 5 and 6, but, unfortunately no specimens from Localities 1 and 4 have yet been tested. Therefore, the following discussion on obsidian sources in Central Anatolia will refer only to Localities 2, 3, 5, and 6 and to Çiftlik.

On the basis of the Na and Mn contents, there is no difference between Localities 2 and 3. These two localities show a clear Na-Mn overlap with Locality 6 (see Fig. 1), although their averages are slightly different. Locality 5, with a mean Mn content of 6.6×10^{-2} per cent (range 6.4 to 6.7×10^{-2} per cent) may be clearly differentiated from Locality 2 (average Mn at 5.1×10^{-2} per cent), 3 (average Mn at 5.0×10^{-2} per cent), and 6 (average Mn at 5.2×10^{-2} per cent). The Çiftlik source has an average Mn content of 6.0×10^{-2} per cent (range 5.8 to 6.2×10^{-2} per cent). Thus, it is lower in Mn content when compared with samples from Locality 5, and has a significantly higher Mn content in comparison with specimens from Locations 2, 3, and 6.

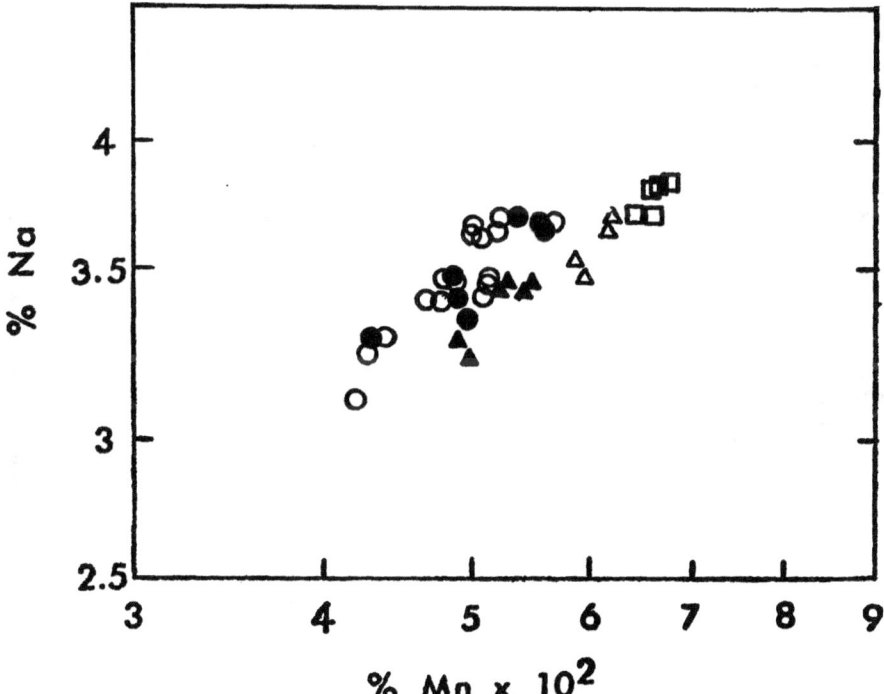

Fig. 1. Sodium and manganese contents of Near Eastern obsidian: Locality 2: ●; Locality 3: ○; Locality 5: □; Locality 6: ▲; Çiftlik: △.

There are virtually no differences in the Na, La, Fe, and Sm contents of these samples. Renfrew *et al.* (1966) have found that Ba and Zr are key elements for separating Acigöl-Topada and Çiftlik. For the former, they computed an average of 648 parts per million (ppm) for Ba and 85 ppm for Zr on five samples. For Çiftlik, they found, as an average for seven specimens, 130 ppm for Ba and 29 ppm for Zr.

We were able to effect a separation on the basis of the data shown in Figs. 1-3 and contained in Tables 2 and 3. These figures illustrate that there is no significant difference between Localities 2 and 3. This is not surprising, as they are located within a few kilometers of each other and could easily belong to the same period of volcanic activity. Localities 2 and 3 show a significantly lower Sc content when compared with the other flows. In addition, their Mn content is also significantly lower than for Çiftlik and Locality 5.

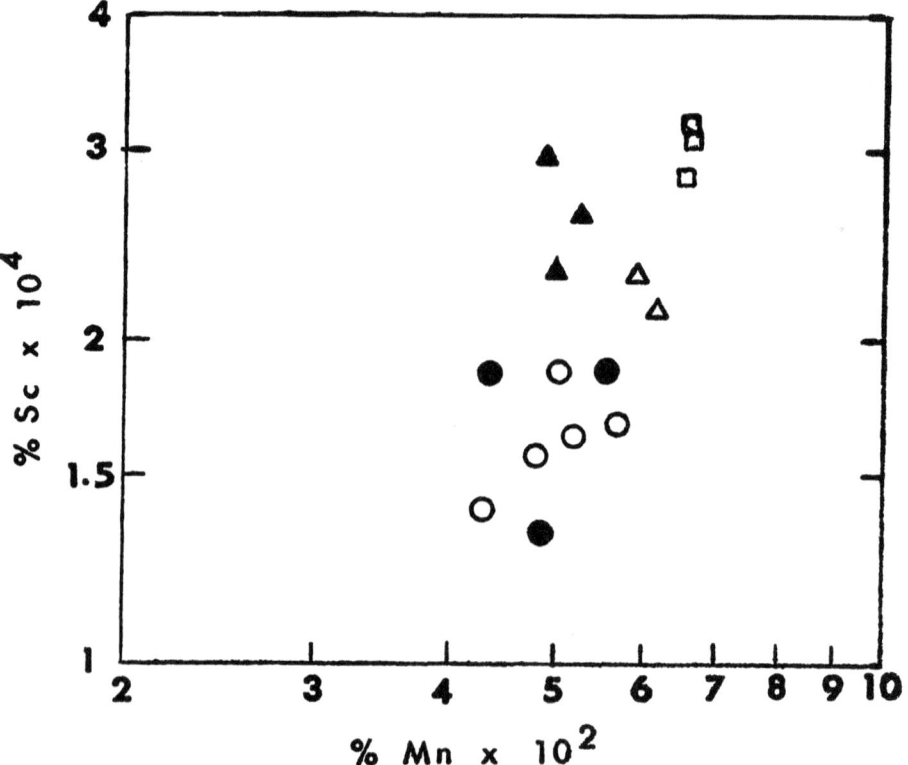

Fig. 2. Scandium and manganese contents of Near Eastern obsidian. Refer to Fig. 1 for identification.

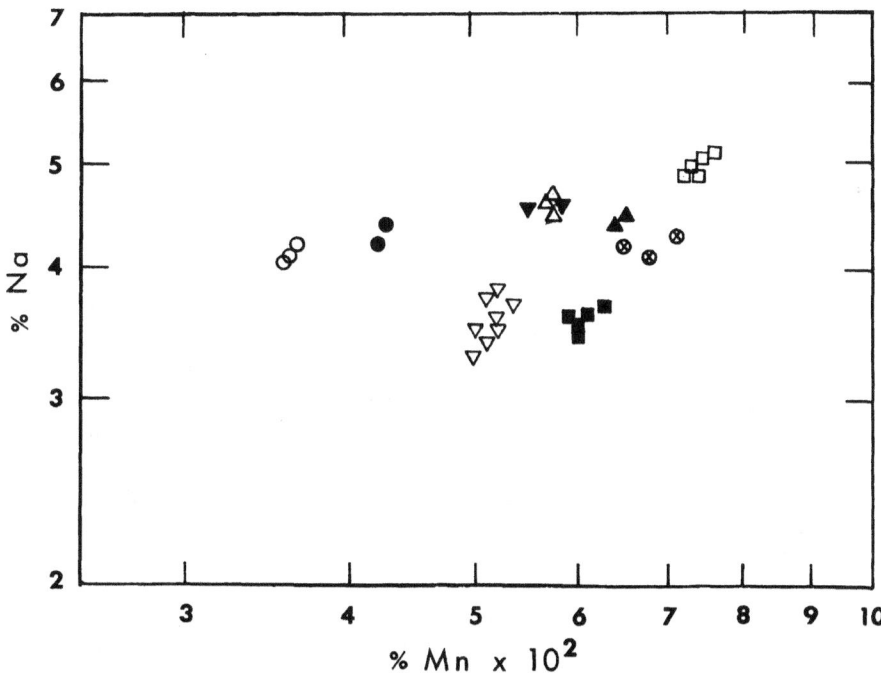

Fig. 3. Sodium and manganese contents of major Near Eastern obsidian groups: □ = Bingöl source; △ = Nemrut Dağ B, 1205-07, Group 4c source; ● = Nemrut Dağ A, 1099-1100; ▲ = Bayezid, 3a source ?; ○ = Group 1g check samples; ▼ = Group 4c check samples; ⊗ = Group 3a check samples; ■ = Çiftlik, Group 2b source; ▽ = Acigöl Locality 3, Group 1e-f source.

Locality 5 has higher Rb and Mn contents than any of the other stations. It also has a high Sc content. In comparison with Locality 5, Çiftlik has significantly lower Rb and Sc. Locality 6 has a higher Sc content than Localities 2 and 3. Thus, on the basis of Mn, Rb, and Sc, these five obsidian localities may be characterized, and, except for 2 and 3, may be differentiated.

Actual sources are less well known in eastern Turkey. The major source flows appear to be located near Lake Van, with the possible exception of a flow near Bayezid, approximately 60 km. southwest of Erevan and 310 km. northwest of Lake Van.

There are at least two separate flows on the Nemrut Dağ. The geology of this area has been studied by Altinli who has recognized 20 separate lava flows. In regard to obsidian specifically he has written: "The material ejected by explosion fell back into the caldera, and together with obsidian, forms small rounded hills. Further east, obsidian lava with intercalations of tuffs consisting of pumice and lava surrounds the andesite cone" (Altinli, 1964: 67-68). The field inspection of Nemrut Dağ by Watson and me in November, 1968, confirmed Altinli's observations that more than one obsidian flow is represented at Nemrut Dağ.

One of these flows is the source for the widely distributed group 4c of Renfrew, Dixon and Cann (1966). Samples from two of the flows may be differentiated on the basis of Mn, Sc, Fe, and Zr. For the first three elements, activation analysis shows clear differences (Table 2), with the Mn and Fe contents of the Nemrut Dağ-B being greater and the Sc content smaller. The data of Renfrew *et al.* (1966: Table II) for samples 82-83 (our 1099 and 1100) give an average Zr content of 405 ppm for Nemrut Dağ-A and for samples 81, 160, and 161 (our 1205-07), an average Zr content of 757 ppm. These latter samples are Nemrut Dağ-B and the data indicate that this particular flow is the 4c group.

The flow near Bayezid may be the source for group 3a. It differs from group 4c in showing a higher Mn content and a Sc concontent which is higher by about a factor of 10. The Sm, Fe, and La contents are significantly lower for the Bayezid specimen (Table 2). It differs from the Central Anatolian sources in its higher Na content. In fact, a preliminary identification may be made on the basis of Na content. All the obsidian samples from Central Anatolian sources have less than 3.8 per cent Na, while the Lake Van source groups have 3.95 per cent Na or larger (Wright and Gordus, 1969).

At least one other important obsidian group (1g) has its most probable source around Lake Van. Group 1g has the highest Na/Mn ratio for any Near Eastern group at 102 to 126. It also shows lower Sm and La contents in comparison to group 4c and a significantly higher Sc content. Judging from the distribution of group 1g site samples, which closely follows the pattern of group 4c, Renfrew *et al.* (1966) have suggested that group 1g ultimately derives also from the Lake Van area. This interpretation is reasonable.

There are several untested obsidian flows near Lake Van. Altinli investigated one flow on Sulphan Dağ which is located just north of and is visible from Nemrut Dağ. "Northwest of Örengazi the andesite of Sulphan occurs as accumulations of basalt block 50 m high, ending in abrupt slopes. Obsidian was ejected during the latest eruptions, preceded by some tuff" (Altinli, 1964: 67).

TABLE 2
ELEMENT CONTENTS OF NEAR EASTERN OBSIDIANS

Sample Number	Location	Per Cent Na	Per Cent Mn $\times 10^2$	Per Cent La $\times 10^2$	Per Cent Fe	Per Cent Rb $\times 10^2$	Per Cent Sc $\times 10^4$	Per Cent Sm $\times 10^3$	Per Cent Na and Mn	Sc/Cs	Sc/Ta	Tb/Cs	Ir/Tb	Ir/Sc	Group
* 676	Central Anatolia Loc. 2	3.24	4.33	0.32	0.97	1.7	1.9	0.63	74.8	...	...	...	...	...	1e-f
* 677	Loc. 2	3.44	4.84	0.42	0.91	1.5	1.3	0.63	71.0	2.0	9.9	3.4	4.4	7.6	1e-f
* 678	Loc. 2	3.65	5.51	0.46	1.2	1.4	1.9	0.76	66.3	...	...	...	...	...	1e-f
* 634	Loc. 3	3.61	5.20	0.62	0.97	1.7	1.6	0.53	69.5	...	...	...	...	...	1e-f
* 663	Loc. 3	3.61	5.01	0.47	1.2	2.1	1.9	0.62	72.1	...	...	...	...	...	1e-f
* 666	Loc. 3	3.46	4.80	0.58	1.0	1.5	1.6	0.57	72.1	...	...	...	...	...	1e-f
* 667	Loc. 3	3.18	4.30	0.50	0.85	1.6	1.4	0.43	73.9	...	...	...	...	...	1e-f
*1114	Loc. 3	3.66	5.71	0.48	1.4	2.0	1.7	0.57	64.1	2.6	15.9	3.3	4.0	5.1	1e-f
508	Munhata 6	3.31	4.55	0.67	1.2	2.2	2.0	0.71	72.7	...	...	...	...	...	1e-f?
* 653	Central Anatolia Loc. 5	3.83	6.73	0.38	0.78	2.3	3.1	0.72	56.9	...	...	...	...	...	...
* 654	Loc. 5	3.81	6.60	0.26	0.95	2.9	3.2	0.60	57.7	...	...	...	...	...	...
* 655	Loc. 5	3.82	6.65	0.26	0.70	2.3	2.8	0.44	57.2	...	...	...	...	...	...
* 656	Loc. 6	3.43	5.26	0.35	0.95	1.3	2.6	0.64	65.1	...	...	...	...	...	...
* 657	Loc. 6	3.17	5.00	0.42	1.0	1.4	2.3	0.44	63.5	...	...	...	...	...	...
* 659	Loc. 6	3.21	4.88	0.58	0.90	1.6	3.0	0.59	65.8	...	...	...	...	...	...
507	El Khiam	3.62	5.18	0.63	0.78	1.5	2.6	0.89	70.0	...	...	...	...	...	...
*1105	Çiftlik	3.67	6.20	0.36	0.70	1.2	2.2	0.68	59.2	2.9	18.2	2.6	3.9	3.4	2b
1106	Çiftlik	3.47	5.96	0.30	0.65	1.5	2.3	0.61	59.9	2.8	16.0	2.4	4.1	3.6	2b

TABLE 2 (continued)

Sample Number	Location	Per Cent Na	Per Cent Mn ×10²	Per Cent La ×10²	Per Cent Fe	Per Cent Rb ×10²	Per Cent Sc ×10⁴	Per Cent Sm ×10³	Per Cent Na and Mn	Sc/Cs	Sc/Ta	Tb/Cs	Ir/Tb	Ir/Sc	Group
516	Munhata 2	3.68	5.86	0.47	0.63	1.4	2.1	0.72	62.8	...	...	...	...	...	2b
517	Munhata 2	3.58	5.94	0.40	0.78	1.6	2.4	0.73	61.0	...	...	...	...	...	2b
630	Munhata 2	3.61	5.80	0.38	0.61	1.4	2.1	0.71	62.2	...	...	...	...	...	2b
687	Mersin	3.55	5.98	0.40	0.77	1.7	2.7	0.72	59.4	2.8	22.8	3.9	4.5	6.2	2b
646	Çatal Hüyük	3.55	5.90	0.65	0.73	1.7	1.1	0.81	60.2	1.6	31.4	3.2	4.5	11.0	2b?
648	Çatal Hüyük	3.36	5.35	0.35	0.97	1.5	1.3	0.61	62.9	...	...	...	...	...	2b?
435	Çayönü	4.41	3.51	0.62	1.8	1.7	3.0	0.86	125.6	3.9	31.3	4.0	4.3	4.4	1g
436	Çayönü	4.00	3.91	0.73	2.5	2.9	4.5	1.1	102.4	...	...	...	...	...	1g
578	Çayönü	4.48	4.31	0.64	1.9	2.6	3.8	0.90	103.5	...	...	...	...	...	1g
682	Çayönü	4.09	3.87	0.68	1.7	1.7	3.3	0.88	105.8	2.7	47.4	2.8	4.7	...	1g
511	Munhata 2	4.19	3.97	0.63	2.4	2.0	3.9	0.89	105.4	...	...	...	...	...	1g
512	Munhata 2	4.18	3.86	0.56	2.0	2.7	3.5	0.80	103.5	...	...	...	...	...	1g
518	Munhata 2	4.24	3.69	0.67	1.7	1.6	3.1	1.0	114.9	...	...	...	...	...	1g
693	Sarab	4.44	4.35	0.80	1.6	2.0	3.5	1.0	102.2	3.9	39.2	2.8	4.6	3.4	1g
717	Jarmo	4.18	3.98	0.71	2.1	2.0	3.5	1.1	105.1	3.0	29.1	2.7	4.1	3.6	1g
1119	Jarmo	4.24	3.70	0.58	1.7	1.8	2.8	0.77	114.6	2.7	27.5	2.5	3.9	3.7	1g
1120	T. Shemshara	4.05	3.53	0.59	1.6	1.8	2.8	0.80	114.7	2.8	31.1	3.4	4.2	4.9	1g
1122	Pulur	4.01	3.57	0.58	1.6	1.6	2.8	0.64	119.9	2.9	29.1	3.3	4.2	4.6	1g
1184	Hazorea	4.10	3.94	0.51	1.6	1.9	2.8	0.56	104.1	...	...	...	...	...	1g
*1208	Bayezid	4.56	6.51	1.0	1.5	1.2	3.1	1.3	70.0	10.3	46.4	9.9	4.1	4.0	3a
*1209	Bayezid	4.49	6.39	0.96	1.7	1.7	3.8	0.96	70.2						3a

OBSIDIAN SOURCES IN THE NEAR EAST

TABLE 2 (continued)

Sample Number	Location	Per Cent Na	Per Cent Mn $\times 10^2$	Per Cent La $\times 10^2$	Per Cent Fe	Per Cent Rb $\times 10^2$	Per Cent Sc $\times 10^4$	Per Cent Sm $\times 10^3$	Per Cent Na and Mn	Sc/Cs	Sc/Ta	Tb/Cs	Ir/Tb	Ir/Sc	Group
1116	Chagar Bazar	4.29	6.60	0.48	1.1	1.2	2.3	0.95	64.9	3.1	17.8	3.6	3.4	3.9	3a
1117	Yanık Tepe	4.10	6.80	0.47	1.2	1.5	2.6	1.1	60.2	2.5	17.5	3.1	3.2	3.9	3a
1118	Arpachiyah	4.28	6.41	0.45	1.2	1.5	2.6	1.1	66.9	2.8	20.9	3.5	3.0	3.6	3a
1149	Banahilk	3.95	6.02	0.56	1.3	1.8	3.3	1.1	65.6	2.9	17.9	3.4	3.7	4.4	3a
595	Ubaid	4.08	4.33	1.3	2.1	5.1	2.8	1.6	92.2						3d
*1099	Nemrut Dağ A	4.26	4.15	0.96	1.6	1.7	1.4	1.7	102.7	1.7	4.8	4.6	2.5	7.3	⋯
*1100	Nemrut Dağ A	4.41	4.18	0.96	1.8	1.4	1.1	1.8	105.5	1.2	4.2	4.5	2.5	9.0	⋯
*1205	Nemrut Dağ B	4.75	5.74	1.5	2.7	1.7	0.47	2.3	82.8	0.37	1.3	6.7	2.3	41.5	4c
*1206	Nemrut Dağ B	4.65	5.70	1.4	2.4	1.5	0.40	2.3	81.6	0.71	2.0	7.2	2.7	27.4	4c
*1207	Nemrut Dağ B	4.57	5.59	1.4	2.6	1.5	0.30	2.4	81.7						4c
587	Ubaid	4.91	6.36	1.5	2.4	1.5	0.35	1.8	77.3						4c
588	Ubaid	4.65	5.85	1.4	2.6	2.0	0.27	1.8	79.5						4c
589	Ubaid	4.71	5.89	1.8	2.4	1.4	0.31	2.4	79.9		0.97				4c
592	Ubaid	4.58	5.80	1.6	2.4	2.2	0.33	1.9	79.0						4c
721	Ubaid	4.24	5.02	1.4	2.7	2.2	0.56	2.5	84.6	0.34		7.7	2.4	53.7	4c
584	Eridu	4.53	5.43	1.4	2.5	1.6	0.31	2.3	83.4	0.39	1.3	6.4	2.2	35.2	4c
434	Çayönü	4.46	5.15	1.3	3.0	1.9	0.31	2.9	86.7	0.22	1.5		2.4	38.3	4c
579	Çayönü	4.38	5.38	1.2	2.3	1.5	0.25	1.8	81.4						4c
706	Ayngerm	4.25	5.19	1.4	2.3	1.6	0.28	2.4	82.4						4c

TABLE 2 (continued)

Sample Number	Location	Per Cent Na	Per Cent Mn $\times 10^2$	Per Cent La $\times 10^2$	Per Cent Fe	Per Cent Rb $\times 10^2$	Per Cent Sc $\times 10^4$	Per Cent Sm $\times 10^3$	Per Cent Na and Mn	Sc/Cs	Sc/Ta	Tb/Cs	Ir/Tb	Ir/Sc	Group
710	Ayngerm	4.49	5.60	1.2	2.3	1.5	0.31	2.2	80.3	...	...	...	...	...	4c
715	Jarmo	4.37	5.55	1.2	3.0	1.6	0.22	2.1	78.8	0.43	1.2	7.9	2.2	42.4	4c
716	Jarmo	4.15	5.25	1.8	3.0	1.8	0.24	2.9	79.2	...	...	...	...	...	4c
694	Sarab	4.57	5.78	1.6	2.2	1.9	0.37	2.9	79.2	0.35	0.92	6.9	2.3	46.6	4c
713	Matarrah	4.21	4.97	1.5	2.7	2.2	0.34	2.7	84.7	0.18	0.50	7.2	2.4	...	4c
712	Ali Kosh	4.43	5.69	1.8	3.0	1.9	0.58	2.9	77.8	...	...	...	...	...	4c
1145	Banahilk	4.35	5.34	1.3	2.2	1.6	0.31	2.1	81.5	0.38	...	7.0	2.5	41.4	4c
1146	Banahilk	4.13	5.04	1.3	2.2	1.5	0.22	2.4	81.9	0.25	0.87	7.0	2.5	71.0	4c
1101	Arpachiyah	4.63	5.73	1.3	2.5	1.7	0.22	2.2	80.8	0.43	1.5	5.9	2.2	30.1	4c
1102	Chagar Bazar	4.52	5.47	1.4	2.5	1.4	0.44	2.3	82.6	0.53	1.7	5.8	2.2	23.7	4c
512	Munhata 2	4.52	5.57	1.7	2.4	1.7	0.46	1.7	81.2	...	...	...	...	...	4c
631	Beisamoun	4.37	5.25	1.7	2.1	1.6	0.39	1.9	77.2	...	...	...	...	...	4c
672	Ramad	4.28	5.49	1.3	2.1	1.4	0.35	1.7	78.0	...	...	...	...	...	4c
*1104	Bingöl	5.10	7.52	1.2	3.1	1.6	0.44	2.1	67.8	0.21	1.2	3.6	2.7	47.3	...
*1131	Bingöl	4.92	7.30	1.6	3.7	2.0	0.35	2.7	68.4	0.22	1.2	3.6	2.3	36.9	...
686	Çayönü	4.91	7.88	1.4	3.5	1.5	0.45	2.5	63.1	0.37	1.2	5.1	2.7	36.4	...
586	Ubaid	4.34	8.04	0.97	0.74	1.3	5.0	0.83	54.2	...	...	...	...	...	...
642	Tilki Tepe	3.79	7.03	0.60	2.4	1.8	1.0	0.97	54.0	...	...	...	...	...	...

Note.—* = Geologic Source.

TABLE 3

SODIUM AND MANGANESE DATA FOR CENTRAL ANATOLIAN OBSIDIAN SOURCES

Origin		Per Cent Sodium	Per Cent Manganese $\times 10^2$	Per Cent Sodium/Manganese
Locality 2	Number	7	7	7
	Average	3.48	5.07	68.6
	Range	3.24-3.67	4.33-5.60	65.0-74.8
Locality 3	Number	15	15	15
	Average	3.49	4.97	70.2
	Range	3.18-3.73	4.30-5.71	64.1-73.9
Locality 5	Number	5	5	5
	Average	3.76	6.59	57.0
	Range	3.66-3.80	6.39-6.73	55.7-58.0
Locality 6	Number	6	6	6
	Average	3.34	5.21	64.1
	Range	3.17-3.43	4.88-5.48	62.2-66.5
Çiftlik	Number	4	4	4
	Average	3.58	6.03	59.4
	Range	3.47-3.67	5.82-6.20	58.2-60.8

Unfortunately, bad weather prevented Watson and myself from collecting samples from this flow.

Obsidian is also known from near Sarakamiş on Aladağ in Kars Vilayet which is located to the north of Lake Van. Samples from this flow are now undergoing analysis in the Michigan laboratory.

Group 3d is represented by only three samples. They show a Rb content around 5.0×10^{-2} per cent. This is the highest Rb content of any of the samples yet tested. The source for this group is still unknown. The three samples are from the archaeological sites of Ubaid, Ras Shamara, and Dahran in Arabia. The distributional data provide no clue as to the source's location.

There is also a flow located about 50 km. east of Bingol. Several samples were tested for Na and Mn. This flow shows a Mn content of about 7.4×10^{-2} per cent; it may be differentiated from group 4c on the basis of Mn contents (Table 2).

The sources for the two geographical foci of major Near Eastern obsidian groups may be differentiated as a whole. Group 4c has one of the lowest Sc contents in the Near East. No sample from this group has yet shown a Sc content of greater than 0.58×10^{-4} per cent. The group 1g samples differ from the Central Anatolian specimens in that the former have a higher Na content, lower Mn content, and a higher Fe content. Thus, the known sources of Near Eastern obsidian may be easily characterized by a variety of elements.

III

OBSIDIAN IN THE NEAR EAST: 7500 TO 3500 B.C.

ALTHOUGH the use of obsidian is seen earlier than 7500 B.C. and later than 3500 B.C., the major period of its most extensive utilization falls between these two dates which roughly define the earliest appearance of settled village communities (though some like Mureybat are earlier) and the end of the Ubaid phase.

First, I will deal with the distribution of obsidian from the two major source areas: Central Anatolia and Lake Van. This will be followed by a discussion of the uses of obsidian in the Near East and will include both the types of artifacts and the amounts of the material found on sites. Finally, I will consider some aspects of the trade of obsidian.

DISTRIBUTION

It was noted above that there were only two major areas of vulcanism in the Near East which contain obsidian flows. As a result, specimens recovered on archaeological sites must have derived from either Central Anatolia or the Lake Van region of eastern Turkey. Element groups 1e-f (Acigöl) and 2b (Çiftlik) have their sources in the former area and groups 4c (Nemrut Dağ), 3a (Bayezid?), 3c (?), and 1g (?) appear to have their sources in the latter region.

In discussing both the distribution and the use of obsidian I will divide the Near East into three subareas: (1) Central Anatolia, (2) the Zagros-Taurus arc and southern Mesopotamia, and (3) (3) Syro-Cilicia and the Levant. Of these three, then, only the latter subarea lacks local obsidian sources.

Central Anatolia

Renfrew and his associates (1966) have defined two element groups with sources in Central Anatolia: group 1e-f and group 2b. The element data were given above. Before considering the archaeological site data, however, some general comments about sources in this subarea will be pertinent. The survey by Benedict (Wright *et al.*, in press) located a number of flows in addition to

Acigöl and Çiftlik. In most cases, chipping debris indicative of
extensive obsidian working was evident at each additional locality.
This suggests that more than two sources were utilized.

The Ba-Zr data from group 2b (both source and sites) were
briefly discussed above. The data in Fig. 4 suggest that either
group 2b obsidian has a very wide range of variation in the contents of these two elements (c. 150 per cent) or that more than one
element group is represented (Wright, n.d.: 37). As most of the
site data fall outside the range of variation for the source values,
I am inclined to favor the latter interpretation.

In order to test this further, we analyzed an archaeological
specimen (1109) from Trebizond (Trabzan) (sample 302 of Renfrew
et al., 1966). We found a Mn content of 4.6×10^{-2} per cent
(Na/Mn = 77.6). This is a significantly lower Mn content than that
of the four analyzed Çiftlik samples given above, and a higher
Na/Mn ratio (Na/Mn for Çiftlik = c. 59-62). It is interesting to
note that the average Sr of the seven Çiftlik samples is 13 ppm

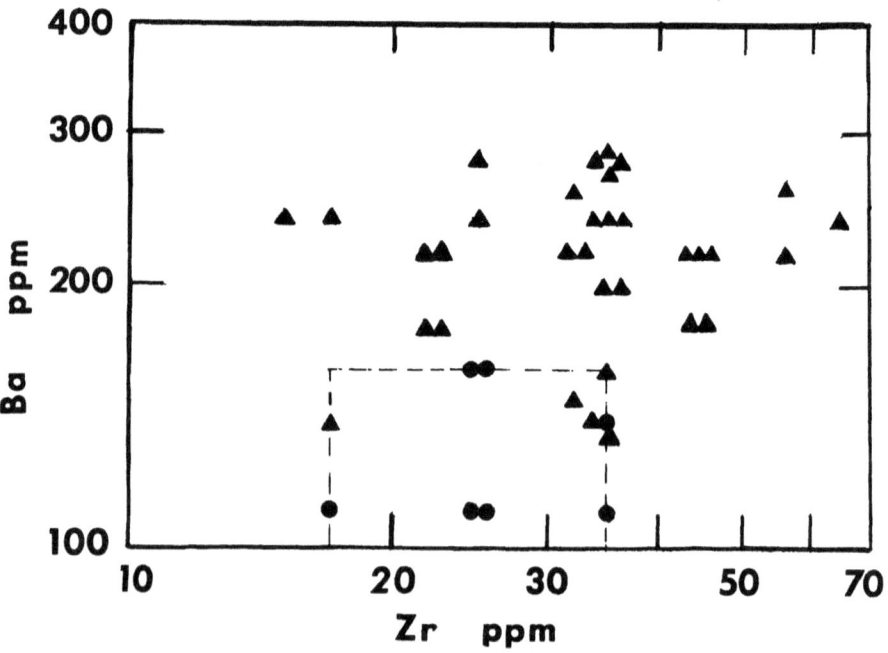

Fig. 4. Plot of barium and zirconium contents for group 2b obsidian: ● =
Çiftlik source samples; ▲ = archaeological samples.

(range less than 10 to 15). This particular sample from Trebizond had a Sr content of 63 ppm and a second specimen (also called 2b) had 120 ppm of Sr. Thus, these two additional elements also indicate that more than one obsidian group may be represented by the 2b samples.

Table 4 gives the Na/Mn data for samples from four sites of this time range in Central Anatolia (Map 2). The Na/Mn ratios of the Çatal Hüyük West (Early Chalcolithic with painted ceramics) specimens are in the group 1e-f range, but the others are closer to group 2b. Samples from Hacilar, Çatal Hüyük, and Çukurkent fell into their group 1e-f.

TABLE 4

SODIUM AND MANGANESE CONTENTS OF OBSIDIAN SAMPLES FROM CENTRAL ANATOLIAN ARCHAEOLOGICAL SITES

Sample	Site	Per Cent Sodium	Per Cent Manganese $\times 10^{-2}$	Per Cent Sodium/Manganese
640	Hacilar II	3.33	5.32	63.0
643	Çatal Hüyük West	3.23	4.52	71.5
644	Çatal Hüyük West	3.38	5.23	64.8
645	Çatal Hüyük West	3.71	5.75	64.5
646	Çatal Hüyük, Neo.	3.36	5.35	62.9
647	Çatal Hüyük, Neo.	3.60	6.02	59.9
648	Çatal Hüyük, Neo.	3.55	5.90	60.2
649	Çukurkent	3.73	6.39	58.4
650	Çukurkent	3.48	5.61	62.1
651	Çukurkent	3.73	6.08	61.3
652	Çukurkent	3.60	5.75	62.8

In Table 2, the additional elements for two specimens from Çatal Hüyük (646 and 648) are given. The Na-Mn data are in the 2b range, rather than 1e-f, but the Sc contents at 1.1 and 1.3×10^{-4} per cent are about one-half of the Çiftlik values for that element. As the Sc/Ta ratio for 646 is higher than the same ratio for either 2b or 1e-f, and the latter have more Sc, it suggests a greater Ta content for the Çatal Hüyük sample. Again, a separate group is very likely.

There is only one sample in this subarea which apparently does not derive from a local source. A specimen (No. 41 of Renfrew *et al.*, 1966) from Çatal Hüyük fits group 1g (Van) most closely. This is a red (oxidized) blade.

20 OBSIDIAN ANALYSES AND PREHISTORIC TRADE

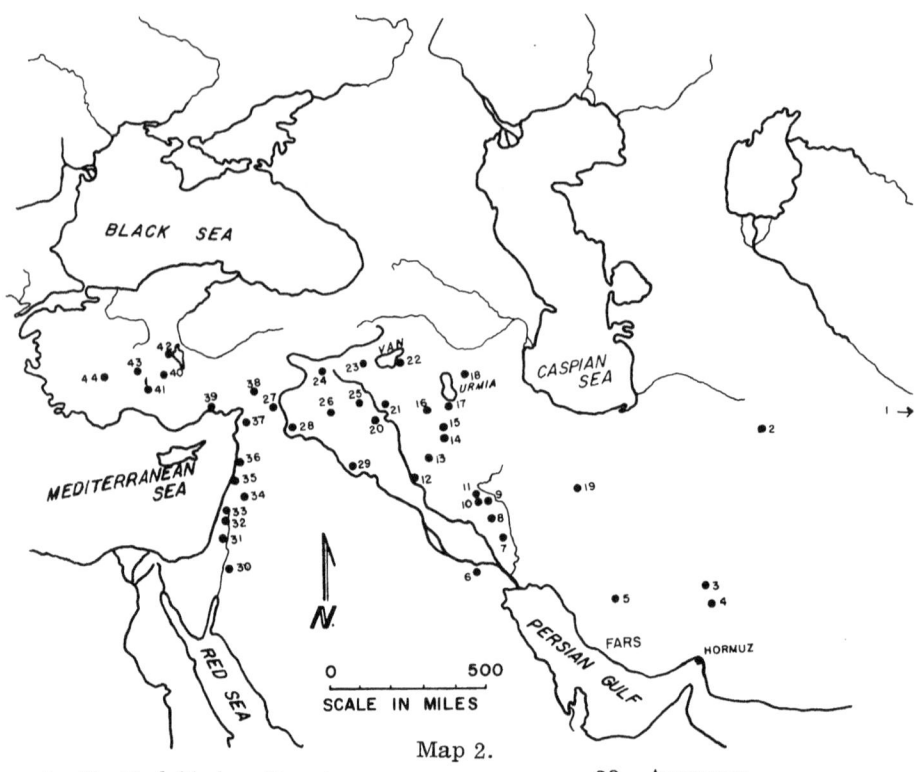

Map 2.

1. To Badakhshan Province
2. Meshed
3. Kirman
4. Tal-i-Iblis
5. Bakun
6. Eridu, Ur, Ubaid Area
7. Ali Kosh, Tepe Sabz Area
8. Tepe Guran
9. Murian
10. Asiab
11. Sarab
12. Tell es-Sawwan, Samarra Area
13. Matarrah
14. Jarmo, Karim Shahir Area
15. Tell Shemshara
16. Banahilk
17. Hajji Firuz
18. Yanik Tepe
19. Tepe Sialk
20. Hassuna
21. Arpachiyah, Nineveh, Tepe Gawra Area
22. Tilki Tepe
23. Ayngerm
24. Çayönü
25. Chagar Bazar
26. Tell Halaf
27. Carchemish
28. Mureybat
29. Bouqras
30. Beidha
31. Jericho
32. Munhata
33. Beisamoun
34. Ramad
35. Byblos
36. T. Hammam
37. Judaidah
38. Sakçe Gözü
39. Mersin
40. Çatal Hüyük
41. Suberde
42. Ilicapinar
43. Çukurkent
44. Hacilar

It should be apparent from the above that I am not yet convinced that only two sources were utilized for obsidian in Central Anatolia. Benedict's survey of the Nevşehir-Aksaray-Niğde region located five previously unreported exposures. This gives, with 2b and 1e-f, a total of seven localities. All of Benedict's localities showed extensive chipping debris (Wright *et al.*, in press).

The element data from archaeological samples also support this position. The source and site data in Fig. 4 from group 2b actually suggest more than one obsidian group. The specimens from Çatal Hüyük tested by us fit no known group. Clearly, there is more work to be done on the characterization and distribution of obsidian groups on the Anatolian Plateau. There is also little reason to suspect that cultural groups in this subarea imported obsidian in any great quantity from the Van region.

Zargos-Taurus Arc and Southern Mesopotamia

Four obsidian groups have their sources around Lake Van. Three of these (4c, 3a, and 1g) I consider to be major groups because of the amount of samples recovered on archaeological sites and their considerable areal distribution (Table 5).

The fourth group (3c) has a very limited distribution. It has been recovered at only 3 sites: Azat (1 sample), Yanik Tepe (5), and Hajji Firuz Tepe (3). Azat is located about 6 kms. east of Kars, about 160 kms. north of Lake Van. The latter two sites are near Lake Urmia, about 130 kms. east of Lake Van. At Yanik Tepe 3c obsidian is found in association with group 3a.

Hijji Firuz has been correlated with Hasanlu X (Renfrew *et al.*, 1966: Table I). The site has two C-14 dates: 5537 ± 85 B.C. (P-455 and 5152 ± 85 B.C. (P-502)). The Azat and Yanik Tepe 3c specimens are Late Chalcolithic and Early Bronze Age.

Groups 4c, 3a, and 1g show a wider distribution and deeper time depth (Wright and Gordus, in press *b*; 1969). The major sites in this subarea for which samples have been tested are given in Table 2. Figures 5 and 6 provide the Na and Mn contents for archaeological samples from this subarea.

A series of interesting observations may be made from the data contained in Figures 5 and 6. There is a break in source utilization which occurs during the Hassuna phase. Prior to this time, the two major sources being utilized in Mesopotamia are 1g and 4c. Samples from these two sources appear in Jarmo, Çayönü, Sarab, Tell Shemshara, Tepe Guran, and in the Deh Luran sites studied by Renfrew (*in*: Hole, Flannery, and Neely, 1969;

TABLE 5

DISTRIBUTION OF OBSIDIAN GROUPS ON MAJOR MESOPOTAMIAN SITES
(Groups Determined by Elemental Analysis)

Site	1g	3a	3c	3d	4c	Bingol	?	Total
Ali Kosh	...	...	...	...	5	...	...	5
Arpachiyah	2	3	...	...	4	...	...	9
Ayngerm	...	...	...	...	5	...	...	5
Azat	...	...	1	...	...	...	...	1
Banahilk	...	4	...	...	7	...	...	11
Çayönü	4	...	...	...	5	1	...	10
Chagar Bazar	...	1	...	...	1	...	...	2
Eridu	...	...	...	...	4	...	...	4
es-Sawwan	...	2	...	...	4	...	...	6
Gawra	...	...	...	...	1	...	...	1
Hajji Firuz	...	...	3	...	...	...	...	3
Halaf	...	1	...	...	...	...	...	1
Hassuna	...	...	...	...	1	...	...	1
Jarmo	5	...	...	...	8	...	1	14
Matarrah	...	...	...	...	3	...	...	3
Sarab	2	...	...	...	4	...	...	6
Tamerkhan	...	...	...	...	1	...	...	1
T. Shemshara	4	...	...	...	2	...	...	6
Tepe Guran	4	...	...	...	4	...	...	8
Thalathat	...	3	...	...	1	...	...	4
Tilki Tepe	...	6	...	1?	3	...	1	11
Ubaid	...	...	...	1	13	...	1	15
Yanik Tepe	...	2	5	...	...	...	...	7
Totals	21	22	9	2	76	1	3	134

Renfrew et al., 1966: Figs. 5 and 6). Ayngerm and Tamerkhan have only group 4c. All of these occurrences date before 5500 B.C.

Only at Çayönü and Jarmo may three groups be recognized. At Çayönü, 4 specimens are group 1g, 5 are group 4c, and 1 is from the Bingol source (Table 2). This is the only certain specimen yet known from Bingol. At Jarmo 5 samples are 1g, 8 are 4c, and 1 belongs to an unidentified group (Renfrew et al., 1966: Fig.5).

Renfrew (in: Hole, Flannery and Neely, 1969) has attempted to separate the specimens from the Deh Luran on the basis of color in transmitted light: grey = 1g and green = 4c. In the Bus Mordeh phase (7500-6750 B.C., Hole and Flannery, 1968) there were a total of 196 pieces of obsidian, all of which were green. The Ali Kosh phase (6750-6000 B.C.) had 578 samples; 72

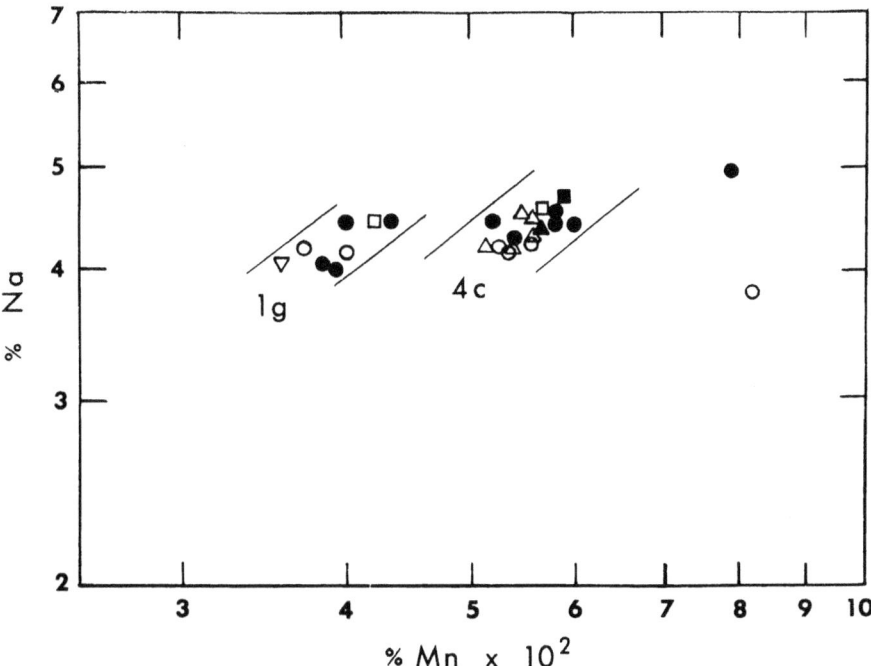

Fig. 5. Sodium and manganese contents of obsidian samples from Pre-Hassuna phase sites: ● = Çayönü; ○ = Jarmo; □ = Sarab; △ = Ayngerm; ▲ = Ali Kosh; ■ = Tamerkhan; ▽ = Tell Shemshara.

were grey (12.4 per cent) and 506 were green. The Mohammad Jaffar phase (6000-5600 B.C.) had 367 specimens; 107 were grey (29.4 per cent) and 260 were green. From the data presented by Renfrew et al. (1966: Table II), however, it is evident that grey obsidian occurs in samples with element contents diagnostic of 4c, and green obsidian is found in group 1g. This method should be used only with extreme caution, and only as a very general indicator of groupings.

In Mesopotamia, the use of group 1g is largely replaced by 3a by the end of the Hassuna phase. Among the earliest occurrences of this group, south of the suspected source area, are at the sites of Banahilk and Tell es-Sawwan. The site of es-Sawwan has yielded Samarran and, reportedly, Hassunan ceramics and C-14 dates of 5506 ± 73 B.C. (P-855) for Level I and 5349 ± 86 B.C. (P-856) for Level III (El-Wailly and Abu es-Soof, 1965). Banahilk is a Halafian phase site and should date about 5100 to 5000 B.C. (Watson, 1965).

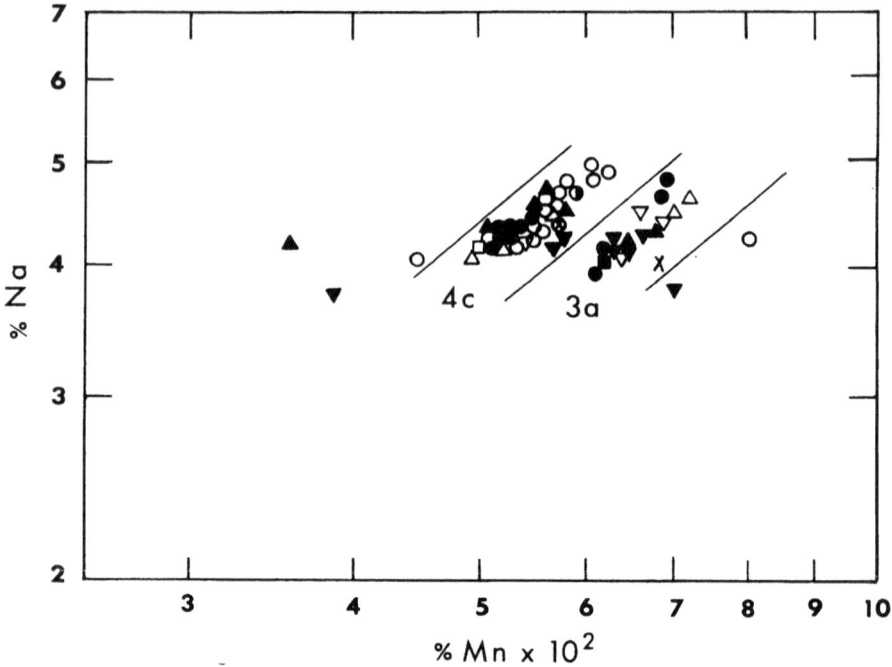

Fig. 6. Sodium and manganese contents of obsidian samples from Hassuna phase and later sites: ● = Banahilk; ○ = Eridu-Ubaid; ▲ = Arpachiyah; △ = es-Sawwan; □ = Matarrah; ▽ = Thalathat; ▼ = Tilki Tepe; ⊗ = Tepe Gawra; ■ = Halaf; ◐ = Hassuna; ✕ = Yanik Tepe.

In Mesopotamia, group 1g appears, on the basis of current data, only at Arpachiyah during the period postdating Hassuna. Here it occurs in association with both groups 3a and 4c.

The beginning of the exploitation of group 3a seems to correlate closely with the earliest occupation of Tilki Tepe. This site is located on the eastern shore of Lake Van where more than 20 obsidian cores (one weighing more than 25 lbs.) and hundreds of obsidian blades were recovered (Pfeiffer, 1940). The site has been interpretated as an obsidian working and trading station. A total of 11 samples have been tested: 6 are group 3a; 3 are group 4c; the final 2 belong to neither group, and are also not group 1g (Fig. 6; Table 2; Renfrew et al., 1966).

From Thalathat, occupied first in Ubaidian times (Egami, 1957), four samples have been tested by activation analysis. Three are group 3a, one is 4c. At Eridu, all four specimens are group 4c.

From Ubaid, 15 samples have been examined by us; 13 are group 4c, 1 is group 3d, and 1 belongs to an unidentified group.

In summary, group 4c was the most extensively used and distributed of the obsidian groups whose sources lie in the Lake Van region. Group 1g, whose source is not yet precisely located, occurs in association with 4c in the Deh Luran by 6750 B.C. and at Çayönü by 7000 B.C. During the Hassuna phase, there is a shift in source emphasis. A new source, 3a, replaced group 1g in Mesopotamia.

There is only one specimen in Mesopotamia which appears to derive from a Central Anatolian source. This is one of the two obsidian vases in Tomb 102 at Tepe Gawra (Tobler, 1950: Plate LIII). It is dated to about 3200 B.C. It is apparently of obsidian from the Acigöl source (1e-f) (Dixon et al., 1968).

Syro-Cilicia and the Levant

There are no natural obsidian sources in the Levant. For this reason, all obsidian recovered on sites must have been traded from either Central Anatolia or Lake Van. In the Levant, no obsidian has been reported from Natufian sites. Obsidian first appears during the Pre-Pottery Neolithic A (PPNA) at Jericho and Nahal Oren. In both cases it makes up less than one per cent of the raw material in the lithic industries. No samples from Nahal Oren have been tested, but 6 specimens from Jericho PPNA were examined by Renfrew and his associates. All 6 fell into their group 2b and are from a Central Anatolian source. They would date to earlier than 7000 B.C. (C-14 dates in Watson, 1965: 85).

During the Pre-Pottery Neolithic B (PPNB), group 2b obsidian is known at Jericho (two samples) and at Beidha (Renfrew et al., 1966; Renfrew personal communication). Three group 2b specimens were found at Beisamoun, and are definitely from the Çiftlik source (Wright and Gordus, in press a; Table 2). At Munhata (Level 6) there is one obsidian microblade. The element data most closely approximate Central Anatolian Locality 3, and the sample is surely from a Central Anatolian source. The large obsidian blade from El Khiam, Level A (Perrot, 1951: Plate XVI, No. 17) was examined by activation analysis; the data most closely fit Central Anatolian Locality 6 (Wright and Gordus, in press a; Table 2).

Obsidian from the Van area first reached the Levant during the PPNB. Group 4c obsidian is known from Beisamoun, Beidha, and Ramad. The Beisamoun data are given in Table 2.

All of the PPNB occurrences should date between 7200 and 6250 B.C. There are seven C-14 dates from Beidha; they range from 6990 to 6600 B.C. (Kirkbride, 1966). PPNB dates from Jericho show a wider range, but there is a cluster between 7220 B.C. and 6250 B.C. (Watson, 1965: 85-86).

Two group 2b blades are known from the Pre-Pottery Neolithic Palace Court III at Ras Shamra on the Syrian coast (Renfrew et al., 1966). C-14 dates place these occurrences at about 6400 to 6200 B.C. (Watson, 1965: 86). We have examined 3 samples from Basal Mersin (C-14 date of 6000 ± 250 B.C., W-617). All 3 had Na/Mn ratios of 59 (Wright et al., in press). This ratio matches Çiftlik. Additional elemental data (Table 2) further suggest the Çiftlik source. Renfrew et al. (1966) have analyzed 7 samples from Mersin; 5 are group 2b and 2 are 1e-f.

Tabbat al-Hamman had two specimens analyzed; both appear to be group 2b (Wright et al., in press). The later (through Ubaid) levels of Ras Shamra and Byblos also have group 2b obsidian (Renfrew et al., 1966), however they also have samples from Lake Van. In fact, five groups are found at Byblos: 1e-f, 2b, 1g, 3a, and 4c.

At Munhata (Level $2A^{1,2,3}$) in the Jordan Valley, 12 samples were recovered. They date to about 4000 B.C. (Perrot, 1967: 12). Four specimens from Hazorea were examined. The level from which the obsidian derives correlates in time with Munhata 2A.

At Munhata 5 samples are 2b, 3 are 4c, and 4 are 1g; at Hazorea, 1 specimen is 2b, 1 is 4c, and 2 are 1g (Wright and Gordus, in press a).

In summary, during the PPNA and PPNB the Çiftlik source in Central Anatolia was by far the most important obsidian source for this subarea. The few pieces at Beidha, Beisamoun, and Ramad do, however, indicate that Van obsidian was reaching the Levant by 6500 B.C. and 4000 B.C., more than one-half of the currently analyzed specimens can be shown to be from Lake Van sources. Although group 1g was extensively utilized in Mesopotamia from 7000 B.C. until the Hassuna phase, it does not make its appearance in the Levant until it was no longer used by prehistoric peoples in the Zagros-Taurus arc and southern Mesopotamia. That is, its utilization in the Levant is post-Hassuna phase in time. At 4000 B.C., group 1g is found in association with groups 4c and 2b at Munhata and Hazorea. Group 3a, as in Mesopotamia, does not appear in the Levant until at least Hassuna times, and probably is slightly later in this subarea.

USES

Central Anatolia

There are now two new preceramic Neolithic sites to add to the aceramic levels of Hacilar. These are Aşikli Hüyük (Todd, 1966) and Suberde (Bordaz, 1966). These sites will provide a general picture of the preceramic Neolithic obsidian industries of Central Anatolia.

Aşikli Hüyük is located in the Niğde Vilayet, approximately 25 km. southeast of Aksaray and 1 km. south of Kizilkaya Köy on the right bank of the Melendiz Çay. Thus, the site is situated in the heartland of the Central Anatolia obsidian sources. The section showed mud brick walls with no traces of stone foundations, traces of red plaster floors, nor fragments of hard limestone. Both animal bones and obsidian are present in large quantities and on typological grounds a date of 7600-7500 B.C. to 6900-6800 B.C. has been proposed with five C-14 dates confirming this age estimate (Todd, 1966, 1968).

The lithic industry was 100 per cent obsidian, excepting the small axes and grinders found on the site. Over 6,200 pieces of obsidian were collected: most of these were tools or tool fragments (for illustrations see Todd, 1966). Obsidian flakes which did not show traces of use were not collected. This is the largest quantity of obsidian yet reported from any site in Anatolia.

Projectile points were comparatively rare in quantity but showed a wide variety of types. Tanged points without pronounced shoulders have retouch restricted to the tang. According to Todd there was one double-pointed arrowhead and a large number of untanged, notched points. Most examples of the latter type have a notch on either side for hafting, though he found a few examples with two notches on one side or with only one side notched. Basal rounded points were rare and all of the recovered single-shouldered points were broken; that is, the point was snapped off. Generally, the tang was partially retouched and there was partial retouch along one side. A considerable number of points on blades were collected.

Blades and blade fragments were present in large numbers at Aşikli Hüyük and "as was the case with the projectile points they display a far greater variety than was found at Çatal Hüyük and other early Neolithic sites" (Todd, 1966: 146). "Heavy knife blades" were recovered in small numbers and from the drawings they appear to show steep backing. Also present were a number of varieties of notched and denticulated blades as well as strangulated blades.

Borers were frequent, both single- and double-ended forms. They were made on flake-blades and blades. Edges on these tools were generally backed. There was one "heavy" double-ended borer and five small examples of this type (Todd, 1966: 147), however, single-pointed borers were more common. There was one crescentic borer and a tool with a borer point at one end and a damaged burin at the opposite end.

Scrapers were numerous. Round, semiround, and oval scrapers have partial to complete steep edge retouch on the upper face. Fan-shaped scrapers vary in shape from "fan- to leaf-shape" and were not as common as round scrapers but were present in large quantities. Other scraper types include sub-rectangular with partial or complete edge retouch, core scrapers, blade scrapers (both single- and double-ended), and nose scrapers.

There are a number of blades which Todd considers to be sickle blades. He found no querns, however, and the only vegetable matter was Hackberry (*Celtis australis*).

Fragmentary cores were recovered but conical blade cores were rare. Core renewal flakes were very common, as were miscellaneous, unretouched flakes.

In summary, the obsidian industry of this site is "characterized by a scarcity of complete unifacial retouch and the total absence of complete bifacial retouch" (Todd, 1966: 140). Predominantly a blade industry, points are few in number but show a variety of forms. Blades and scrapers are present in large numbers and burins, borers, cores, and sickles(?) are present. A large quantity of flakes exhibiting retouch and/or use were also collected.

The site of Suberde is located 11 km. southeast of Seydişehir. It is situated on a ridge, locally called Görüklük Tepe, along Suğla Lake. There are three levels at the site. Level I is Islamic and need not concern us here. Levels II and III are Early Neolithic; Level III has a C-14 date of 6570 ± 140 B.C. (I-1867). Thus it is earlier than Çatal Hüyük X and probably correlates with Aceramic Hacilar.

Only a two page report has been published on the site, yet in this short paper Bordaz (1966) provides the preliminary tool counts. About 90 per cent of the industry was on obsidian; unfortunately there are no data on source(s). The excavation resulted in 2500 tools, 230 cores and core fragments, 3200 blades and flakes with retouch, and 24,000 waste flakes.

Unifacially pressure-flaked points were the most common tool type (455 examples). Other important tool forms include: circular scrapers (282), sickle blades (100), notched pieces (100), reamers and fragments (93), blades with alternate retouch (76), side scrapers (54), and micro-tools (45) (Bordaz, 1966: 31).

Other artifacts collected were 63 small celts and other polished stone tools and beads and pendants, 40 bone piercers, and a piece of copper wire and copper ore. Although 25,000 animal bones were recovered, apparently none show osteological evidence of domestication.

The preceramic levels of Hacilar date to about 7000 B.C. and are partly contemporaneous with Aşikli Hüyük. Interestingly, a total of only 5 pieces of flint and 2 of obsidian were recovered in the several years' excavations of the preceramic levels of this site (Todd, 1966: 160).[1] Thus there are no comparative data here.

The earliest ceramics reported from Central Anatolia derive from Çatal Hüyük. Mellaart (1967) has uncovered 13 separate building levels, all showing ceramics. A C-14 date (P-782) dates Level X to 6142 ± 98 B.C. and one (P-779) from Level IX to 6240 ± 99 B.C. (Stuckenrath and Ralph, 1965) (5570 year half-life). Thus, it appears that occupation at the site began late in the second half of the seventh millennium B.C., or using the 5730 half-life (as does Mellaart) slightly before 6500 B.C.

Analysis of the lithic industry (1337 specimens) collected from the earlier phases of the excavations was undertaken by Bialor (1962). About 95 per cent of the industry (this includes the latest total) is obsidian (Dixon et al., 1968). Buff chert was used chiefly for large side scrapers, one sickle blade, and four projectile points according to Bialor's study which concentrated on hunting equipment.

Projectile points (132) dominated the homogeneous industry and were found in nearly every room (Levels VIII-II). Most projectile points were tanged (108); 78 of the 108 tanged forms were unshouldered and were bifacially retouched. There were 23 unshouldered, unifacially retouched, tanged points. Only 24 of the 132 points were untanged Six of the untanged forms were bifacially retouched, double-pointed types, 9 were bifacially retouched with rounded bases, and 5 were other bifacially retouched forms. In all, 103 of the 132 points were bifacial. This is a marked contrast to the preceramic industry from Aşikli Hüyük.

---

[1] In October, 1968, Dr. Richard A. Watson and I collected about 25 obsidian blades from the surface of the Hacilar mound. Both flint and obsidian are abundant on the surface.

Blades (692) and flakes (336) make up the bulk of the lithic industry studied by Bialor. Other important tools were scrapers (91), piercers (29), daggers (26), cores and core fragments (22). All other forms have less than 20 examples. There is an almost total absence of microliths, with only a few atypical examples in obsidian having been recovered from Levels II and III (Mellaart, 1967: 214).

Cores and blanks occurred in hoards. It is evident, then, that knapping was done on the site, not at the source. Piercers and borers were rare; according to Mellaart their place was taken by bone awls.

Obsidian was also utilized for less utilitarian objects. Obsidian mirrors and beads were recovered, often with female burials. There were two caches of leaf-shaped obsidian knives with about a dozen examples in each cache and a triangular obsidian pendant (Mellaart, 1964: Pl. XXV c).

In summary, there are a number of marked changes evident at Çatal Hüyük even though obsidian was still the principal raw material in the chipped-stone industry. Bifacial retouch predominates in the projectile points in contrast to Aşikli Hüyük. Still, like Aşikli Hüyük, hunting must have played an extremely important part in the life of the Neolithic people of Çatal Hüyük. Nearly the entire chipped-stone industry, the projectile points and lances in the hunt itself, daggers and knife blades in butchering and the scrapers and borers in the preparation of pelts and skins might be accounted for in this activity alone (Bialor, 1962: 71).

There are also new forms and uses of obsidian. Mirrors, beads, and pendants are fashioned in this material and are included as grave goods. Finally, worked points are also utilized as grave furniture; for example, the male burial in House E, VI B, 20, (c. 5700-5600 B.C.) had 8 obsidian projectile points.

There are other Neolithic sites with obsidian industries similar to Çatal Hüyük. The site of Ilicapinar is located 12 km. south of Cihanbeyli on the main road from Ankara to Konya; the small mound lies slightly east of the village near the northern end of the salt lake, the Acituz Gölü. Mellaart collected 89 finished or broken obsidian tools and 215 chips and flakes. Predominant are bifacially flaked, tanged projectile points very similar to the points from Çatal Hüyük. In fact, Mellaart (1958: 92) said of his initial collection from Çatal Hüyük: "The obsidian is absolutely identical with that of Ilicapinar."

Obsidian of a roughly contemporary age comes from the Çukurkent group near the lake of Beyşehir (Mellaart, 1954; 1958).

Leaf-shaped, bifacially flaked points occur. Obsidian blades were common at all the Çukurkent sites. In short "there seems to be little difference, if any, between the obsidian of Ilicapinar and that of the sites of the Çukurkent group" (Mellaart, 1958: 88), although ceramics were collected from the latter sites.

By Çatal Hüyük II the stone industry becomes "debased" (Mellaart, 1965 b: 100). Obsidian is more sparse in Late Neolithic and Early to Middle Chalcolithic levels. For example, the stone industry is poor in numbers and types at Hacilar. There is, however, a novel usage of obsidian at this site. In Level I (c. 5000 B.C.) there are a number of hollow effigies or anthropomorphic vessels in the form of a seated goddess; the largest is a foot tall. They were fashioned on red-on-cream ware "and the eyes, and sometimes the ears, brow, nose, and chin were inlaid in obsidian" (Mellaart, 1960: 103, Pl. XV a-s). One figurine in Level I had an inlaid obsidian navel.

Obsidian occurs in the Middle Chalcolithic at Çatal Hüyük West. At the latter site Mellaart (1965 a: 136) writes of "a poor blade industry in obsidian." The Can Hasan obsidian industry has not yet been described in detail, although French (1966) has recovered a fair quantity of flakes and blades in several years of excavations.

From the Bronze Age Hittite capital of Boğazköy there is a toilette table of Egyptian workmanship, bearing the cartouche of the Hyksos ruler Chian. A small flake from the same site proved to be of Egyptian origin, group 4d (Renfrew *et al.*, 1966: 49).

To summarize, obsidian in archaeological sites appears to be predominantly of local origin. The use of obsidian seems to begin in the Paleolithic. There is a hand axe at Avla Dağ (Todd and Pasquare, 1965: 112) and in Aurignacian IV levels at Öküzini and Karain; the latter are from group 2b (Renfrew *et al.*, 1966: 43). It is not until about 7500 B.C., however, that obsidian predominates as the major raw material in the lithic industries of Central Anatolia. The best analyzed complex of tools in preceramic times comes from Aşikli Hüyük as given above. The first major change is seen at Çatal Hüyük, Ilicapinar, and the Çukurkent group with an emphasis on projectile points which are bifacially worked. Points at Aşikli Hüyük make up only 2.5 per cent of the industry. More exotic uses of obsidian are found at Çatal Hüyük by Level VI (c. 5700-5600 B.C.) such as mirrors, beads, and pendants, and in Level I at Hacilar in the form of obsidian inlays in figurines. According to most investigators, by the Early Chalcolithic (the end of the sixth millennium B.C.) the obsidian industry becomes impoverished.

Zagros-Taurus Arc and Southern Mesopotamia

There are more excavated sites in this subarea pertaining to the time period under consideration than for either of the other two subareas. Similarly, percentagewise, there are fewer published accounts of chipped-stone industries which contain counts of tool types and raw materials. In many cases where sites have been reported, the lithic material was discarded at the site (uncounted), remains in a museum (in Baghdad or elsewhere with the descriptions not yet available) or is in manuscript form but still unpublished. The lack of concrete data will be very evident in this section.

The earliest obsidian artifacts in this subarea are said to be of Middle Paleolithic type from eastern Turkey (Renfrew et al., 1966: 40). There are two pieces of obsidian from Shanidar in Level C (groups 4c and 1e-f), a dozen pieces in Level B (L. Braidwood, 1961), and two samples from Zarzi Cave; one of the latter is group 4c (Renfrew et al., 1966: 42). It is about 450 km. from Nemrut Dağ to Zarzi.

Obsidian appeared in the Deh Luran in the Bus Mordeh phase around 7500 B.C. In this phase, the excavations by Hole and Flannery recovered 196 pieces of obsidian. This is about 1 per cent of the lithic material (Hole and Flannery, 1968: 173) and it is presumably all group 4c (Renfrew, in: Hole, Flannery, and Neely, 1969). In the Ali Kosh phase (6750-6000 B.C.), there were 578 pieces of obsidian, about 2.5 per cent of the lithic material. In the Mohammad Jaffar phase (6000-5600 B.C.) ceramics first appear. The obsidian count drops to 367 pieces (1.5 per cent). Obsidian was absent in the excavations from the succeeding Sabz (5500-5000 B.C.) and Khazineh (5000-4500 B.C.) phases but reappeared in the Mehmeh phase (4500-4100 B.C.). It was used for blades and constituted less than 1 per cent of the chipped-stone tools (Hole and Flannery, 1968). Obsidian, again, made up less than 1 per cent of the lithic material in the Bayat phase (4100-3700 B.C.).

The Deh Luran obsidian industry is quite uninspired. Blades and chips were recovered, but exotic items were lacking. Even at a time period when obsidian vases appear to the north, they were absent in the Deh Luran.

To the north, in Luristan, obsidian was quite common in certain levels at Tepe Guran (Mortensen et al., 1964). Occupation at the sites began slightly before 6500 B.C. and continued until at least 5000 B.C. The lowest level, V, had 2 per cent obsidian and Level U had 0 per cent (Renfrew et al., 1966: 58). In Level T, about 6350 B.C., 36 of the 80 pieces of stone (46 per cent) were obsidian. This level is the high point, percentagewise, for obsidian at this site. It then reduced to 6 per cent in Level S and 0 per cent in Level R; but in Levels P, O, and N the percentages of obsidian were 22, 45, and 20, respectively. After this point, it never reached above 11 per cent.

In regard to the obsidian percentages at Tepe Guran, it should be noted that no level had more than 170 pieces of chipped stone. Thus, as the Ali Kosh phase had 23,231 pieces of stone, the comparative Tepe Guran figure should be used with caution.

Again, the industry was predominantly based on blade production. No exotic obsidian forms have been reported and we still await the final tool tabulations.

In Kurdistan and Luristan, Braidwood has located and/or excavated an impressive number of early village sites over the last 20 years. In the earlier sites (e.g., Asiab, Karim Shahir, M'lefaat, and Gird Chai), which date between 7000 to 8000 B.C., less than six pieces of obsidian were found in each site (Braidwood, personal communication).

The Jarmo and Sarab chipped-stone industries have been subjected to an intensive analysis by Hole (n.d.). Tables 6 and 7 give various categories of obsidian usage at the two sites (Hole, n.d. and personal communication). The preceramic phase at Jarmo will date to about 6750 B.C., the ceramic levels to about 6000 B.C., and Sarab may be overlapped in part by ceramic Jarmo and should date to about 5900 B.C. (c. 6000-5600 B.C.) (Mortensen, 1964).

It may be seen in Table 6 that obsidian was frequently used at Jarmo (and recall that three sources are represented), while at Sarab, although 628 pieces of obsidian were recovered, it represents only 1.7 per cent of the total chipped stone. In unit X (J-I), preceramic Jarmo, 28.1 per cent of the chipped stone is obsidian. Obsidian was preferred for blades, microliths, and Hole's miscellaneous category (Table 7). About 45 per cent of the tools and 51 per cent of the blades in Unit X were fashioned on obsidian.

In Unit Y (the ceramic phase at Jarmo) the total obsidian percentages jumps to 45 per cent. About 68 per cent of the tools and 75 per cent of the blades are of this material. At nearly contemporary Sarab, however, only 4.8 per cent of the tools and 5 per cent of the blades were obsidian. The factors behind this difference will be discussed below.

Hole (n.d.: 112-16) has summarized the chipped-stone industry at these two sites as follows. There was more flint debris at Sarab than in either Jarmo phase; there were relatively more flint

TABLE 6
PERCENTAGES OF OBSIDIAN AT JARMO AND SARAB

Analytic Unit	Total Stone	Total Obsidian	Per Cent Obsidian	Total Tools	Obsidian Tools	Per Cent Obsidian	Total Blades	Obsidian Blades	Per Cent Obsidian
Y (JII-1)	23,945	12,005	50.2	...	...	...	...	...	...
-2	21,178	9,751	46.1	...	...	...	...	...	...
-2⊥	11,486	5,257	45.8	...	...	...	...	...	...
-3	9,432	4,085	43.4	...	...	...	...	...	...
-4	6,124	1,900	31.0	...	...	...	...	...	...
-5	8,919	3,515	39.5	...	...	...	...	...	...
-6	4,408	1,979	44.8	...	...	...	...	...	...
X (JI-6)	6,196	2,075	33.5	...	...	...	...	...	...
-7	5,318	1,587	29.8	...	...	...	...	...	...
-8	10,183	2,436	23.9	...	...	...	...	...	...
Z (SI-C)	40,864	723	1.7	13,035	628	4.8	11,530	604	5.2
Y JII	85,492	38,492	45.0	37,310	25,490	68.3	35,607	26,869	75.4
X JI	21,697	6,098	28.1	11,581	5,260	45.4	8,949	4,566	51.0

Note.—Y (JII-) = latest (ceramic) occupation at Jarmo; X (JI-) = earliest (preceramic) occupation at Jarmo; Z (SI-C) = one-third of total excavated area at Sarab.

TABLE 7

PERCENTAGE OF OBSIDIAN IN EACH TOOL GROUP
AT JARMO AND SARAB

Analytic Unit	I	II	III	IV	V	VI
Y (J-II)	71	18	70	37	3	86
X (J-I)	61	17	46	26	2	91
Z (Si-C)	...	...	5	1	1	35

Note.—I = microprojectile elements (e.g. trapezes, triangles, and other geometries); II = piercing-reaming tools; III = cutting-scraping tools; IV = end scrapers; V = side scrapers; VI = miscellaneous (e.g. burins, fabricators, etc.).

tools than debris in Unit X at Jarmo than in Unit Y; and far less obsidian debris was recovered in any unit relative to flint. The latter observation suggests that obsidian was traded in as finished blades, whereas flint was brought onto the site in raw form, and blades were struck at the site.

This hypothesis is supported not only by the relative absence of obsidian debris, but also by the fact that no obsidian cores were recovered. In contrast, in Jarmo Unit Y there were 24 blade cores, 346 flake cores, and 744 core fragments of flint (total 1114), and in Jarmo Unit X there were 22 blade cores, 68 flake cores, and 223 core fragments of flint (total of 313) (Hole, personal communication).

In Unit Y at Jarmo there was a greater use of obsidian for blades in comparison to Unit X (75 to 51 per cent). In all units "obsidian was used mainly for blades, whatever its frequency relative to flint" (Hole, n.d.: 116).

According to Hole's (n.d.: 112) analysis, "obsidian was used for more types of tools in Unit Y than in Unit X . . . and in no case was obsidian used on types in Unit X that it was not also used on in Unit Y." In contrast at Sarab, obsidian was utilized for only 8 of the 39 tool types defined by Hole.

To the northwest of Jarmo there is a final preceramic Neolithic site which may be mentioned. This is Çayönü, which is located in the Diyarbakir Vilayet of southeastern Turkey, near the town of Ergani in the Tigris drainage. The site is C-14 dated at about 7000 B.C.

No report is available as yet (and thus no tool descriptions), but the stone has been studied by Peter Benedict. I was able to obtain the counts from Dr. Braidwood and they are given in Table 8. The percentage of obsidian steadily rises from less than 20 per cent at the bottom to nearly 50 per cent by the end of the pre-ceramic occupation.

TABLE 8
ÇAYÖNÜ OBSIDIAN

Level	Total Stone	Obsidian	Per Cent Obsidian
Square 5-6			
Sur-1	2,076	1,033	49.1
1-4	802	287	35.8
4-5	5,686	990	17.4
Square 8-9			
Sur-1	679	295	43.4
1-4	482	167	34.6
4-5	2,008	367	18.3
Grand Total			
Sur-1	2,755	1,328	48.2
1-4	1,284	454	35.4
4-5	7,694	1,357	17.6
	11,733	3,139	26.7

There are a number of sites from the Hassuna phase (c. 5800-5200 B.C.) from which obsidian has been reported. The site of Matarrah, 34 km. south of Kirkuk, has two ceramic phases: Samarran-Hassuna in the upper levels, and Hassunan in the lower (Braidwood, et al., 1952). Smith (in Braidwood et al., 1952) studied about 40 per cent of the chipped stone. In the lower levels, of the 848 pieces of chipped stone, 74 (8.7 per cent) were obsidian. In the upper levels 56 (23 per cent) of the 188 pieces were of this material. Blades and borers predominated and there were no obsidian cores.

No counts are available from Tell Hassuna, which is located 22 miles south of Mosul (Lloyd and Safar, 1945), however, obsidian did occur. The industry was based on blade production, but is "by and large, a wretched affair" (Braidwood, 1967: 121).

Tell es-Sawwan is a Hassunan-Samarran site and is located on the eastern bank of the Tigris, 11 km. south of Samarra. Obsidian was present in all five levels. As noted above, two groups, 3a and 4c, have been recognized; it is the earliest known 3a occurrence. The obsidian industry consists predominantly of sickle blades, borers, core-scrapers, and knife blades. There was one fragment of a sickle which incorporated one obsidian and three flint blades; they were held together with bitumen. In Level I (room 141) there was an infant's grave; grave goods included one obsidian blade, a plate, a cup, a bowl, and a bone needle (for illustrations, see El-Wailly and Abu Es-Soof, 1965).

At Yanik Tepe, near Tabriz, the obsidian industry was composed mostly of blades. The early phase at the site dates from about 6000 B.C. into the first half of the sixth millennium B.C. (Burney, 1964). There is also a later Chalcolithic occupation. Burney has suggested that there may be a local obsidian source at Mount Sahend. As group 3c obsidian is present on the site, and the source has not yet been located, Burney's suggestion remains a possibility. He also suggests that the site is located near an alabaster source (Burney, 1964: 56).

There are a number of excavated sites dating to the Halafian and Ubaidian phases. The Halaf phase is generally understood to correlate in northern Mesopotamia with the southern Mesopotamian Ubaid 2. The Halaf phase began at about 5200-5100 B.C. The Ubaid phase ended at about 3500 B.C. There are no useful tool counts for any of these sites at present, however, a number of new forms of obsidian objects occur and these are generally acknowledged in the reports. The new forms include bowls, beads, and pendants.

At Banahilk (Halafian at c. 5000 B.C.) apparently none of these exotic forms were present (Watson, 1965). Blades and notched blades did occur but no counts are yet available (Braidwood and Howe, 1960: 34). Both groups 3a and 4c were present.

The earliest occupation at Tilki Tepe seems to be Halafian. Located on the eastern shore of Lake Van, it is in the center of the Van obsidian source area and lies directly across the southern end of the lake from Nemrut Dağ. Large cores and hundreds of blades were recovered. It seems to have served as an obsidian trading station. Both groups 3a and 4c were present as well as at least one unidentified source.

Levels 15-7 at Chagar Bazar date from the Samarran through the Halafian phase; all northern Ubaid is lacking (Mallowan, 1936,

1937). This site is one of the earliest tells in the Khabur River region. During historic times this tell lay on the overland caravan route from the Habur to the upper Tigris. In prehistoric times, according to Mallowan (1936: 7) this was a much frequented route connecting Harran, T. Halaf, T. Has (a large prehistoric mound in the Wadi Way), T. Chagar Bazar, T. Hamidi, and T. Furfara. In short, the entire region was covered by a series of caravan routes which connected the towns of northern Syria with Nineveh and the prehistoric centers of Assyria. According to the Babylonian texts described by Gadd (1937), it was also an important grain producing center.

Obsidian was common in all prehistoric levels at Chagar Bazar but became rarer as the Chalcolithic progressed. Obsidian blades were found with bitumen still adhering. An obsidian bead was found in Level II. Levels 7 and 8 also produced Persian Gulf shell (*Cyraea vitallus*) and other exotic items which will be noted in the next section.

In his Balikh Valley survey, Mallowan (1946) tested Tell Aswad. The site is situated on the east bank of the Nahr al Turkman, a branch of the Balikh. It was abandoned at the end of the Halaf period. He excavated one house and an ox skull was found lying in the doorway. There are no obsidian counts but Mallowan does comment that obsidian was found in a small quantity in comparison to chert (Mallowan, 1946: 156).

There are three sites in the northern portion of this subarea which contain both Halafian and northern Ubaid ceramics: Arpachiyah, Sakçe Gözü, and Tepe Gawra. Sakçe Gözü is located about 30 miles northwest of Gaziantep in southeastern Turkey (Taylor *et al.*, 1950). Although the chipped-stone industry is not well described, counts were provided by the investigators and are given in Table 9. Obsidian, apparently, was not too common,[2] reaching its highest percentage at 12.3 per cent during their Samarran-Early Halaf level. Most of the chipped-stone tools were fashioned on dark brown to light grey chert which was readily available in the limestone hills two or three miles from the site. Only two pieces of obsidian are described: one had two opposing notches at one end and at the opposite end it was retouched into an end scraper.

There were 10 stratigraphic levels at Arpachiyah: TT 1-4, Ubaid; TT 5, Ubaid-Halaf; TT 6, Climax Halaf; TT 7, Developed

---

[2] Dr. Richard A. Watson and I were able to find only one obsidian flake on the surface of this mound in October, 1968.

TABLE 9
OBSIDIAN AT SAKÇE GÖZÜ

Level	Total Stone	Obsidian	Per Cent Obsidian	Period
I	121	12	9.9	Pre-Halaf
II	114	14	12.3	Samarran-Early Halaf
III	87	2	2.3	Developed Halaf
IV (A-C)	174	12	6.9	Ubaid
IV-A	30	0	0	
IV-B	32	2	6.3	
IV-C	112	10	8.9	

Tholoi; and 8-10, Early Halaf (Mallowan and Rose, 1935). No counts of obsidian and flint tools are given. The authors, however, state that they recovered thousands of flint and obsidian knives and scrapers and that obsidian "was quite as common as flint" (p. 102).

They found numerous obsidian cores which indicates that obsidian blades were struck at the site. Other tools include a scythe-shaped blade with a short tang.

In TT 6, there were a number of kilns in the center of the site. One house in TT 6 has been identified by the authors as a potter's shop. One room had stone vases, jewelry, cult figurines, amulets, and flint and obsidian tools. Lumps of red ochre and painter's palletes were found lying on the floor beside painted pottery. A number of cores and chips were recovered; the authors also suggest that a specialized knapper may have been present (p. 105).

There were also new uses of obsidian. In TT 6 there was an obsidian vase and a necklace of long flattened obsidian double conoid beads which were pierced longitudinally; between them were cowrie shells, the backs of which were cut away and filled with red paint (Mallowan and Rose, 1935: 97, Pl. XI, a, Pl. VI, c).

In addition, Mallowan and Rose collected a series of rectangular obsidian "links," perforated at the ends, sometimes twice and sometimes four times. All of the beads were recovered in the same room.

In the use of many nonlocal raw materials, and a long stratified sequence, Tepe Gawra (Tobler, 1950) is very similar to Arpachiyah. Here we will deal mainly with the Area A and the Northeast Base and Levels XX to XII (c. 5000 to 3500 B.C.). Again there are no counts, but Tobler (p. 201) estimates that in all but

XVI, more than 50 per cent of the implements are of obsidian. It should be noted, however, that he found (or saved) very few stone implements in the lower levels (e.g., XV was barren). Speiser (1935: 84) states that there was "a very large number of unregistered duplicates."

In Area A (pre-Level XX) there was 1 obsidian blade, 1 scraper, and 2 suspension-hole pendants. From the Northwest B Base (also pre-XX), Tobler recovered 3 different "ornaments" of this material: one is a disc-shaped pendant which is characterized by two suspension holes set closely together. An example of this type of pendant is illustrated by Tobler (Pl. CVII, Fig. 52) and is from Tomb G 36-135 and is attributed to stratum XI.

Peculiar to Area A and the Northwest Base was a variety of obsidian described as chocolate brown in color. Obsidian with a "greenish tinge" predominates in the upper levels. A "smokey" obsidian first appears in Level XIII.

In strata XIX to XVI at Tepe Gawra, obsidian, white paste, carnelian, limestone, and marble were employed for making beads. By Level XIII turquoise, amethyst, lapis lazuli, agate, quartz, jadeite, beryl, diorite, haematite, steatite, and serpentine are added to the bead raw material inventory. In Level XVII, in graves, loci 7-52, 4J and 7-57, 3J, obsidian beads were found with burials. They will date to approximately 3900 to 4000 B.C.

About one-half of the tanged pendants with engraved and drilled decorations were fashioned from marble. Other popular materials were serpentine and black steatite, with "no more than eight specimens having been made of quartz, obsidian, haematite, and amethyst" (Tobler, 1950: 195). The obsidian tanged pendants fall, for the most part, between levels XVI and XII.

There were lozenge-shaped pendants of obsidian, having a single suspension hole. One was found in stratum XV and one in stratum XIII. The suspension-hole pendant from XVI was mentioned above; the same level also produced three blades and two scrapers of obsidian.

There were 9 ornamental studs with ornamental borings. Seven were made of obsidian. Three come from the Northwest Base, 2 from XVIII, 1 from XVI, and 1 from VIII or IX.

Seals first appear in XIX and come into extensive use in stratum XIII. Two-thirds derive from strata XII, XI-A, and XI. Most of the Gawra seals are on stone: steatite, serpentine, lapis lazuli, agate, carnelian, haematite, and obsidian. According to Tobler (1950: 176), none of these stones are native to Mesopotamia and had to have been imported. Mellaart (1965*b*: 130-31) suggests

Badakhshan, at the foot of the Pamirs (Afghanistan), as the source area for all these materials, except obsidian. Three obsidian seals are illustrated by Tobler (1950: Pls. CLXVII, Figs. 135 and 139; CLXX, Fig. 181). One is a gable-shaped seal, another a hemispheroidal seal of obsidian from XI, and the third a hemispheroidal-shaped seal from XII.

Although the obsidian bowl and jar were found in an adult burial (Tomb 102) dating from Level X (c. 3200 B.C.), and thus in a strict sense out of the time range of interest here, they may be briefly mentioned. Tobler also suggests that they may have been made earlier and were heirlooms. The bowl (Tobler 1950: Pl. LIII c and Fig. 7) is extremely well-made, apparently of obsidian from a Central Anatolian source (Dixon et al., 1968: 38). The spouted jar is 10 cm. in height and 11.6 cm. in diameter. The spout and part of the rim had been broken and repaired by boring five pairs of holes, each hole connected with grooves with thongs holding the fragments in place.

There are fragments of obsidian bowls from both Shahrain and al-Ubaid which date to the Ubaid phase. The fragments of obsidian beakers found between Levels C and D of the Anu Ziggurat at Warka are attributed by Perkins to the Ubaid phase "on the basis of shape . . . and because of the use of obsidian which is rare after the Ubaid period" (Perkins, 1949: 86).

In the connection of more exotic uses of obsidian, the Late Chalcolithic levels of Yanik Tepe are of some interest. The ceramics are comparable to the Late Chalcolithic of the Hasanlu area, particularly as represented by Dalma Tepe. A date of 4036 ± 87 B.C. (P-503) was obtained at the latter site. The upper levels of Yanik Tepe show distinct parallels in ceramics with Pisdeli Tepe and date to the mid-fourth millennium B.C. (Burney, 1964: 58).

A form of ceramic decoration, unique to this site, is a schematized rendering of the human face below the rim of a bowl with flakes of translucent obsidian. The flakes are set into the openings through the entire thickness of the bowl to portray the eyes. This bowl was recovered in a rubbish dump in Level MB 5. Other examples comprise only the two eyes, with no attempt to portray the nose or eyebrows.

Further to the south, at Ras al 'Amiya, located five miles north of Kish, midway between the Tigris and Euphrates, Stronach has excavated a site containing Hajji Muhammad ceramics (Ubaid 2) "mitigated as they are by some Samarran as well as Halaf motifs" (1961: 123). Obsidian was common but counts are not available. The obsidian industry was predominately small blades, however, in House 5, Level III, a "fish-tailed" obsidian object was recovered.

Obsidian is known from Ubaid and Eridu. We have run more samples from Ubaid than any other Near Eastern site. Unfortunately, the chipped-stone assemblages from these sites still await description. During the autumn of 1968 I was able to collect obsidian specimens from Early Bronze levels at Çayönü, Korucu Tepe, and Tepecik. The latter two are sites in the Keban Reservoir area of southeastern Turkey, about 100 km. west of Çayönü. The samples are now undergoing analysis in the Michigan laboratory.

Levant and Syro-Cilicia

One of the earliest occurrences of obsidian in this subarea is at Mureybat; unfortunately none of these samples have yet been tested. The site, located on the Middle Euphrates in Syria, showed XVII levels. There are two C-14 dates from Level I (the lowest level) 8142 ± 118 B.C. (P-1216) and 8056 ± 96 B.C. (P-1215); one date from II is 8256 ± 117 B.C. (P-1217); a single date from X-XI is 8018 ± 115 B.C. (p. 1220); one date from XVI is 7542 ± 122 B.C. (P-1222) (van Loon, 1966: 216).

The economy was apparently based on the intensive collecting of wild cereals (barley and einkorn) and the hunting of wild cattle (30 per cent), onager (30 per cent), gazelle (30 per cent) and fallow deer, boar, wolf, and hare (10 per cent). Clay vessels were absent but stone bowls were present.

About 70,000 pieces of chipped stone were collected. Heavy tools were made on flint and chert cores and flakes. "The light tool kit is essentially the same as that of the Upper Paleolithic about 40,000 years ago" (van Loon, 1966: 214). Obsidian was rare and first appeared in the eighth level from the bottom. Counts and descriptions of obsidian tools are not yet available.

To the south of Mureybat is a second prepottery Neolithic site: Bouqras. Data on the obsidian was provided for Renfrew et al. (1966: 59) by M. Henry de Contenson. Level I is preceramic and correlates with preceramic Jarmo; there were 173 pieces of obsidian (32.3 per cent of the industry). Level II is also preceramic; 295 obsidian samples were recovered (25.7 per cent). Level III (a ceramic level) had 151 pieces of obsidian (27.9 per cent). The chipped-stone industry is not yet described. Both groups 1g and 4c are represented (Dixon et al., 1968).

There was no obsidian in the Natufian or Proto-Neolithic

levels at Jericho. In the PPNA 344 of the 11,884 pieces of chipped stone were obsidian (2.9 per cent) (Renfrew *et al.*, 1966: 61). In the PPNB, 60 of the 4944 pieces of chipped stone were obsidian (1.2 per cent). In contrast to Munhata and Hazorea there was no obsidian recovered from the Pottery Neolithic.

Obsidian occurred in Level I (PPNA) at Nahal Oren which is located just south of Haifa and was also found in Level II (PPNA) (Stekelis and Yizraely, 1963: 2, 7). According to Renfrew and his associates (1966: 61) "in structure 10 of Stratum II . . . obsidian blades form 1 per cent of the total lithic assemblage."

There was only one obsidian blade from the PPNB at Munhata, Level 6. Four pieces of obsidian were collected from the surface at Beisamoun (PPNB). They include two blades, one retouched flake, and one scraper. The single specimen from El Khiam Level A (c. 6500 B.C.) is a large utilized blade (Perrot, 1951). It measures 5.0 cm. in length and 1.2 in width.

In Munhata 2A (c. 4000 B.C.) there were 12 pieces of obsidian (less than 1 per cent). There were 5 microblades, 2 retouched microblades, 4 blades, and 1 retouched flake. There were 4 obsidian blades tested from Hazorea (c. 4000 B.C.).

Two preceramic levels were excavated at Ramad. The excavators recovered 21 pieces of obsidian in Level I (the lowest) and 57 in Level II (1.1 per cent and 0.7 per cent respectively) (Renfrew *et al.*, 1966: 61). The samples are not yet described.

Unfortunately, we still lack the complete tool descriptions from the important site of Ras Shamra. Contenson (1963) does indicate, however, that obsidian appears in the earliest preceramic level, V C. This level is dated to the first half of the seventh millennium B.C. There is a pre-pottery C-14 date of 6414 ± 101 B.C. (P-460). Contenson believes that the flint and obsidian blade industry at this site is related to the earliest Syro-Cilician materials and possibly to the obsidian industry at Çatal Hüyük.

The chipped-stone industry of Basal Tabbat al-Hamman has been studied by Hole (1959). This assemblage is datable to the Amuq A-B phases and will date to the early sixth millennium B.C. There were 322 pieces of chipped stone, with about 5.2 per cent being obsidian. There was one obsidian point, a point fragment, and 15 blade sections.

The tool counts from Phases A-E (Early Neolithic through the Ubaid equivalent) for Tell al-Judaiah in the Amuq are given in Table 10 (Payne, *in* Braidwood and Braidwood, 1960). At all times more than 18 per cent of the chipped stone is on obsidian. Blades, blade sections, and nibbled blades predominate in all levels.

TABLE 10
OBSIDIAN AT TELL AL-JUDAIDAH

Phase	Points	Borers	Gra-vers	End Scrapers	Side Scrapers	Nibbled Blades	Blades	Blade Section	Flakes	Renewal Flakes	Core Tab.	Cores	Misc.	Total	Total Stone	Per Cent Obsidian
E	...	2	1	5	4	*	8	176	24	...	...	...	10	230	699	33
D	...	...	...	...	...	*	...	9	7	...	...	1	...	17	70	24
C	...	...	...	...	...	*	2	35	6	...	...	1	...	44	122	36
First Mixed	...	...	...	...	...	6	13	32	4	2	...	2	1	60	327	18
A–B	4	2	...	...	...	31	48	267	39	9	2	14	6	422	1,732	24

*Included under blades or blade sections.

TABLE 11
OBSIDIAN PERCENTAGES FROM 1946–47 MERSIN EXCAVATIONS

Levels	Blades	Sickle Blades	Borers	Scrapers	Notched Scrapers	Rejects	Used Flakes	Points	Cores	Total Stone	Per Cent Obsidian	Period
XVI–XX	29.1	0	0.9	2.0	1.7	43.1	7.5	0.5	1.7	1,214	87	Middle Chalcolithic
XXI–XXIV	31.5	0	3.7	1.6	0.7	33.9	5.0	0.4	0	1,191	77	Early Chalcolithic
XXV–XXVIII	34.7	0	3.8	1.0	0.6	30.6	11.2	2.6	0	631	84	Neolithic

Points (4) on obsidian occur only in Phases A-B and side (4) and end scrapers (5) only in Phase E. There are 49 obsidian beads which date to the First Mixed Range.

The Mersin obsidian counts are given in Table 11 (Bice, *in* Garstang, 1953). The industry is not well described. There are a number of point types similar to those at Çatal Hüyük. In Levels XXIX to XXVII there are numerous pressure flaked, tanged points. Both unifacially and bifacially worked points are common; other obsidian tool types in these levels include borers, daggers, scrapers, "slugs," and backed blades. Sickle blades are on chert. In Level XXIV, Garstang (p. 30) notes that there is little or no change in the industry, except that sickle blades become more numerous. Level XXIV is termed "Proto-Chalcolithic." According to Garstang (p. 52), obsidian becomes less common and varied; there are now numbers of long, narrow, untrimmed obsidian blades. Levels XXIII-XX show predominately borers, blades, and scrapers; points are nearly absent. By Level XIX, obsidian is limited almost entirely to flakes (Garstang, 1953: 106). The only obsidian cores from the Neolithic through the Middle Chalcolithic levels come from Level XVII, where four were recovered.

Stratified finds of obsidian in the Neolithic levels were rare at Tarsus but an "immense" number of obsidian flakes were found by Goldman (1956: 256), who indicates that there were no implements characteristic of contemporary levels at Mersin which were found *in situ*, but they were found unstratified and out of context. According to Goldman, the Chalcolithic levels were nearly barren of implements.

TRADE AND TRANSPORT

In this section I wish to consider some significant points about the movement of obsidian during this time period and will discuss a Locational Analysis Model recently proposed by Renfrew (in press). This quantitative model has led to some interesting conclusions on Renfrew's part and is worthy of detailed examination.

First, it will be useful to draw together certain aspects of the distributional and usage data outlined earlier in this chapter, and to present some brief comments on obsidian trade and transport. Because the obsidian sources (or source areas as for group 1g) are discoverable by elemental analysis, the possibility of contacts between any two specific areas may be established with some degree of accuracy. Thus, even though obsidian was often not too important a raw material in regions far removed from the source (e.g., in the Deh Luran), hypotheses about prehistoric cultural development which include "culture contact" as one variable, may in certain cases be examined in the light of information about the movement of obsidian.

For example, Harlan and Zohary (1966: 1079) from their study of wild wheats have recently suggested that "the present evidence indicates that most modern tetraploid cultivated wheats stemmed from the [wild] race now found in the upper Jordan watershed." The crucial time period in the domestication of wheat and its spread out of its natural habitat zone is about 7500 to 6500 B.C. By 6500 B.C. domesticated wheat was known at Beidha (Helbaek, *in* Kirkbride, 1966) in Jordan, at Jericho (Flannery, personal communication), and in the Zagros-Taurus arc. We also know that Van obsidian, group 4c, was traded into the Levant by 6500 B.C., as it appears in PPNB contexts at Beidha, Beisamoun, and Ramad (Wright and Gordus, in press *a*). With these obsidian data, there is now evidence from three separate sites in the Levant that prehistoric groups in Palestine and the Zagros-Taurus arc were in contact by 6500 B.C. Even if this contact was only indirect, as seems most probable, a route from the movement of early domesticated wheat was established. Viewed in this respect, the few pieces of 4c obsidian in the Levant take on new significance.

Unfortunately, the Van obsidian sources have not yet been thoroughly investigated. Prior to the Halaf phase, cores are not reported from the major sites, and it seems likely following Hole's (n.d.) conclusions from the Jarmo and Sarab data, that obsidian was transported outside the source area in the form of blades and not as cores.

Tilki Tepe is first occupied during the Halaf phase. As mentioned above, large cores and hundreds of obsidian blades were recovered from the site, which is situated in the heart of the Van obsidian source area. Tilki Tepe has been interpreted as an obsidian working and trading station. Both the important 4c and 3a groups were found in the analyses, but not 1g.

Still we can not categorically state that from the Halafian phase onward, obsidian was only transported in the form of blades. There are two reasons for this statement: (1) We have cores reported from a "workshop" at Arpachiyah, and (2) The large number of beads, seals, etc. which appear by the Ubaid phase were not fashioned from blades. Therefore, it was also moved from the Lake Van sources in the form of unprepared blocks or as cores during the Halaf and Ubaid phases. Perhaps this is due to the development of efficient water transportation.

In connection with the obsidian trade, two features stand out at Arpachiyah. First are the cores, and second is the fact that Arpachiyah is the only known post-Hassuna phase site in northern Mesopotamia with group 1g obsidian. It is approximately at this time that group 1g goes out of usage in northern Mesopotamia, but makes its initial appearance in the Levant. This site, with all three Van obsidian groups represented, seems to be a focal point for the movement of Van obsidian into the Levant.

Obsidian working stations are known from each of the Central Anatolian source localities investigated by Benedict (Wright *et al.*, in press). It appears that some initial preparation of the material was done right at the source. Yet, "cores, roughouts, and raw material occur in hoards" at Çatal Hüyük, "showing that fabrication was done on the site" (Mellaart, 1967: 214). There were 230 cores and core fragments recovered at Suberde (Bordaz, 1966). At Aşikli Hüyük, fragmentary cores and core renewal flakes were common (Todd, 1966). They are not mentioned, however, for Ilicapinar and the Cukurkent group sites (Mellaart, 1958), nor for Hacilar.

I have a feeling that it is only on the surface that there is an apparent difference between the utilization of the Van and Central Anatolian sources. Note that the sites like Çatal Hüyük, etc., where cores occur, are all within 300 km. of the Central Anatolian sources, but Hacilar lies well beyond that limit. This 300 km. radius from the source has been termed a "supply zone" by Renfrew (in press; see also below). The same kind of data from sites within 300 km. of the Van sources are rare. There appears to be a limit as to how far bulk obsidian may be economically transported; the preparation would thus be different for obsidian to be transported from the supply zone, that is, as blades rather than cores.

The mechanisms by which the material was actually moved between groups is still another problem. Let me point out here that obsidian was only one material which was being exchanged, and in areas far from the sources (e.g., the Jordan Valley) it was never too important a commodity. In this respect, a consideration of the trade mechanisms by which obsidian was moved is by itself too narrow a view. It must of necessity be considered in conjunction with other goods.

The Renfrew Model

Renfrew (in press) has proposed that the study of prehistoric exchange systems be approached by quantitative analysis. He has suggested and has applied to his obsidian studies a "movement lapse rate" model (Haggett, 1965: 34-35) currently employed by locational and economic geographers. This model considers the movement of goods in relation to the distances involved: that is, the *amount* of goods and the *distance* the goods must be transported.

The amount (here the per cent obsidian in the lithic assemblage) is plotted on a log-log or log-linear graph against distance (in km.) from the edge of the source (or source area as the Van region or the Nevşehir-Aksaray-Niğde triangle) (Renfrew, in press; Dixon *et al.*, 1968: 45). From this type of graph (Fig. 7 is an example), Renfrew deduces the following conclusions on the Near Eastern obsidian trade: (*a*) within a distance of approximately 300 km. of the supply zone, sites were well supplied with obsidian between 7500 and 5500 B.C. as this raw material formed about 80 per cent of the chipped-stone industry; and (*b*) outside the supply zone, the per cent of obsidian falls rapidly. As the points do not fall on a straight line (see Dixon *et al.*, 1968: 45), the fall-off in supply is not exponential with distance, but drops proportionally to the fourth or fifth power of the distance from the supply zone (Renfrew, in press).

This model then has a number of advantages for the presentation and the description of the movement of goods, particularly, as expressed quantitatively. I find some problems in the exact mechanics of the model, however, as conceived by Renfrew and also with some of his conclusions.

1). Rather than the percentage of obsidian samples in the lithic assemblage, a more important consideration would be the weight of the samples. This is particularly so when dealing with a stage of cultural development where pack animals were probably lacking and the transport of goods was by human agency, though model boats are known from the Ubaid (Lines, n.d.). In this type of situation, it was not the *number* of items to be transported but how much they *weighed*. Thus, in assessing the obsidian in a chipped-stone industry by weight, an obsidian core weighing 15 lbs. would not be counted the same as a blade weighing less than 0.1 oz. There is a considerable difference in transportation decisions if the results of the trade are 50 per cent of the lithic assemblage being ultimately microlithic tools of obsidian rather than large obsidian ceremonial blades.

Weight is a difficult factor with which to deal for the Near Eastern lithic assemblages excavated in the past because: (*a*) samples like blades were often never counted; (*b*) chipping debris was ignored almost entirely; (*c*) there has been little screening of

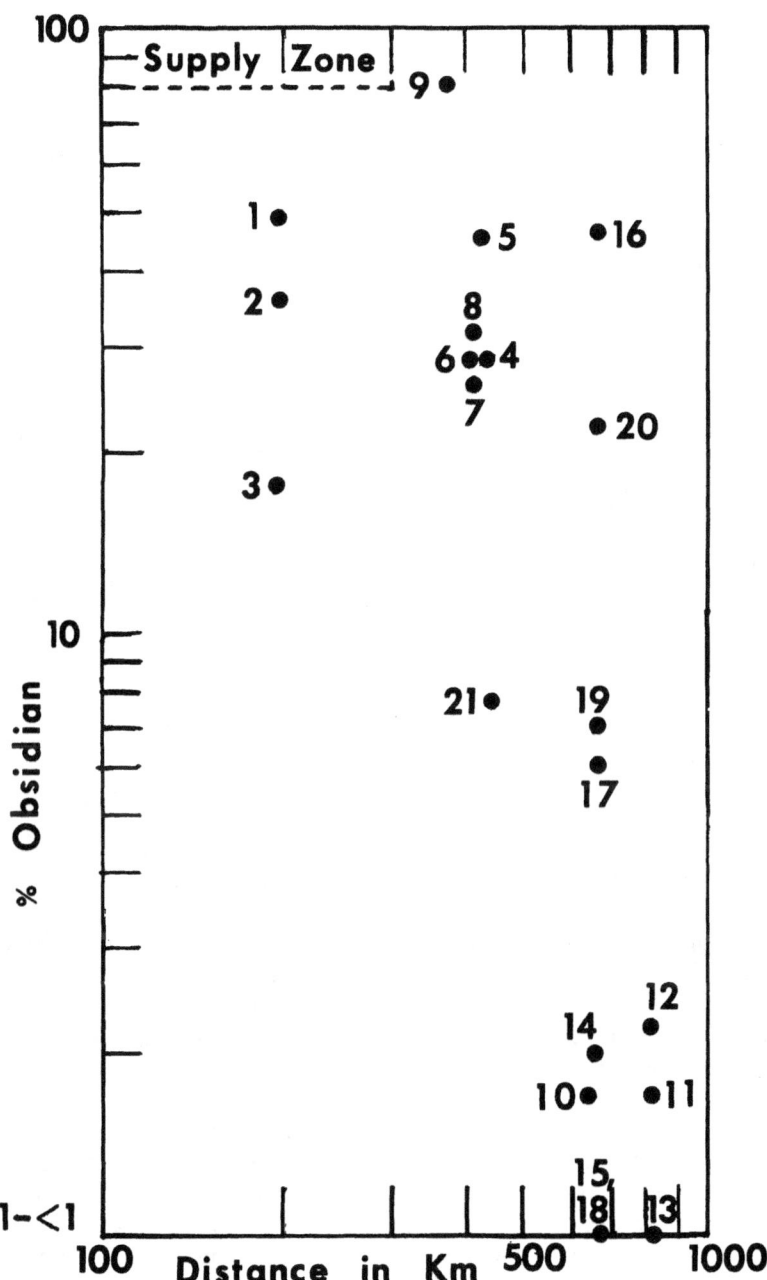

Fig. 7.

Fig. 7: Plot of distances from Van sources and percentages of Obsidian on archaeological sites.

Site and Level or Phase	Percent Obsidian	Distance (km.)
1. Çayönü, Sur.-1	48.2	195
2. Çayönü, 1-4	35.4	195
3. Çayönü, 4-5	17.6	195
4. Jarmo II	45.0	415
5. Jarmo I	28.1	415
6. Bouqras III	27.9	410
7. Bouqras II	25.7	410
8. Bouqras I	32.3	410
9. Tell Shemshara, 16	81	365
10. Sarab	1.7	650
11. Ali Kosh Mohammad Jaffar	1.7	815
12. Ali Kosh, Ali Kosh	2.1	815
13. Ali Kosh, Bus Mordeh	0.9	815
14. Tepe Guran, V	2	675
15. Tepe Guran, U	0	675
16. Tepe Guran, T	46	675
17. Tepe Guran, S	6	675
18. Tepe Guran, R	0	675
19. Tepe Guran, Q	7	675
20. Tepe Guran, P	22	675
21. Matarrah, Lower Levels	8.7	450

material; and (d) the forms of obsidian usage changed through time so that a weight estimate per sample for one site at 7000 B.C. can not be applied indiscriminately to a second site dating to 4000 B.C. In regard to the latter point, where the sites are not functionally equivalent (e.g., herders' encampment and farmers' village), even when they occur in the same area (like Luristan) at the same time, the weight per sample constant probably will not hold true due to different functional requirements of the tools.

Renfrew, himself, has had to reevaluate his weight estimate for Jarmo. In an earlier paper (Renfrew et al., 1966: 52) he estimated that 4000 kg. (4 tons) of obsidian was brought into Jarmo. This was based on a figure of 4 kg. per 1000 pieces as a mean weight; this constant was derived from his study of obsidian from the Neolithic site of Saliagos in the Cyclades. Since examining the Jarmo samples personally, he now feels that a more realistic figure is 20 gm. per 1000 pieces, and thus a total weight of 196 kg. (Renfrew, 1969). This is a considerable weight reduction.

2). The generalizations mentioned above which Renfrew derived from his graph seem to hold strictly only for the Central

Anatolian supply zone and not for the Van sources. In Figure 7, I have replotted the obsidian data for sites in the Zagros-Taurus arc between 7500 and 5500 B.C. I have made some changes in presentation, however, and added data not available to Renfrew (e.g., Çayönü).

In contrast to Renfrew, I have not considered an entire site as one datum point, but have plotted the individual levels or phases: for example, Jarmo I and Jarmo II are plotted separately. Thus, rather than saying that 10 per cent of the chipped stone at Tepe Guran is obsidian, I have plotted levels P-V individually (Fig. 7).

Only one site within the Van supply zone, Çayönü, has obsidian counts. Theoretically, according to the model, the percentages of obsidian should be 80 per cent or higher. For the three analytical units, however, they are from top to bottom: 17.6, 35.4, and 48.2 per cent respectively. Thus, they fall well below their predicted value.

Based on the predictive model (Dixon et al., 1968: 45), no level at Tepe Guran should show more than 7.5 per cent obsidian. Yet, the site has about a 10 per cent value when all levels are considered as a whole. When plotted by individual levels, both Levels T and P fall well above the 7.5 per cent limit at 46 per cent and 22 per cent, respectively (Fig. 7).

3). A further problem arises when functionally nonequivalent sites are compared indiscriminately. If we take, for example, Murian, Tal-i-Iblis, Sarab, Tepe Guran, and the Yunus Kilns at Carchemish, we have a series of sites which appear to differ in function: flint production, copper production, nomadic herders' encampment, settled farming village, and pottery production. In this situation, one would, first of all, not expect the same lithic tool types to be present. Second, the ratio of obsidian to flint on each of these sites would expectably vary: in fact, even though nomad encampment of Sarab is closer to the obsidian supply zone than the village of Tepe Guran, most levels at the latter site show more obsidian than was recovered at Sarab. This is probably due to the tasks performed at each site; that is, the differences are functional. Renfrew has suggested that site inaccessability is a primary factor; but considering the mobility of nomads, this seems to be of less importance than the use to which the material was put.

4). A fourth factor is the availability of local flint resources. The model appears to work best for the Central Anatolian sites, where naturally occurring "obsidian is abundant, but flint is absent" (Mellaart, 1967: 16). In contrast, flint is found in eastern Turkey. Being locally available, it was utilized apparently as consistently as was obsidian to judge from the Çayönü data. Thus, if one wishes to use percentages, adjustments are necessary for the assumptions behind the predictive model for the Van region supply zone, in contrast to the situation in Central Anatolia where natural flint is apparently absent.

IV

NEAR EASTERN TRADE: 7500 TO 3500 B.C.

FOR THE most part, "trade" to the archaeologist has meant "long distance trade" and more specifically "long distance trade in luxury items." When only this type of trade is considered, however, the possibly more significant local trade may be overlooked entirely. Take, for example, the case presented by Downs and Ekvall (1965) on Tibet: while the long distance specialized trade should produce nonlocal artifacts which would be apparent in the excavations, the more local exchanges of food products (specific to the nomadic and farming groups) might be missed. Thus, the archaeological investigator might end his report with erroneous conclusions about the economy, adaptation, and social relationships of the prehistoric groups under consideration. He would be able to determine that external relations were carried on through long distance trade, but the important local movement of food products, as a separate trade system, would not be apparent if only artifacts were studied. This is an important consideration to keep in mind when analyzing prehistoric Near Eastern trade.

By the sixth millennium B.C. there is evidence to indicate that herding as a seasonal, if not full-time, occupation was being practiced. These herders are important for two reasons: (1) they must operate in some form of exchange system to trade their specialized products from their animals for goods they do not produce, like grain, and (2) today, and presumably in the past, they are a vehicle for the movement of certain commodities.

In this respect, it is also clear that by the reign of Sargon I (c. 2300 B.C.) a vigorous and active long distance trade was being carried on by specialized traders, both overland to Lebanon and Central Anatolia and across the sea to India (Adams, 1966). It is this trade to which Mallowan (1965) addressed himself in his article "The Mechanics of Ancient Trade in Western Asia." This approach is comparable to ignoring the local market trade of the Aztecs and focusing only on the activities of the *pochteca*. It is clearly only part of the story.

It is, of course, easier to deal with long distance trade in archaeological situations where written records of local economies are absent, because exotic nonlocal raw materials will readily stand out among the artifacts. We have, for example, turquoise from northeastern Iran in the Mohammad Jaffar phase in the Deh Luran by the early sixth millennium B.C. (Hole and Flannery, 1968: 179). We have evidence of the long distance movement of obsidian even earlier.

When it comes to more local trade, the data generally must come from a study of local subsistence economies. But the relevant data are lacking for the most part. We must ask, and are hard put to answer: (1) What subsistence or ecological specialties are represented within or between valley systems by the sites and their artifacts during the preceramic, Hassuna, Halaf, and Ubaid phases? (2) What craft specialties are represented on specific sites?

With these warnings in mind, I wish to look at the changing pattern of trade in the Near East between 7500 and 3500 B.C. As for obsidian, the data are very poor for certain areas, even though considerable work has been done. There are no economic or quantified data for large and important sites like Tarsus, Chagar Bazar, Arpachiyah, Tepe Gawra, and many others. In some respects, I shall be pointing out what we do not know, or what we should know, in order to make this exercise successful, rather than providing answers to the questions raised.

SOURCES OF OTHER RAW MATERIALS

Before beginning our analysis it will be useful to indicate briefly some of the suspected sources for many of the raw materials. In some cases, like obsidian, this is quite easy; for other raw materials, like copper, it is more difficult, if not impossible at present, to indicate exactly which source produced a given copper artifact.

The two major source areas for obsidian have been discussed in detail elsewhere in this work. There is apparently only one major lapis lazuli source area. Mellaart (1965 *b*: 130-31) lists the province of Badakhshan at the foot of the Pamirs in Afghanistan as the region from which lapis was derived. One specific source has been investigated by Lapparent *et al.* (1965: 30). It is located at Sar-i-Sang in the Hindu Kush (Afghanistan) at an elevation of 2450 m. Hermann (1968) lists four lapis mines in this area: Sar-i-Sang, Stromby, Chilmak, and Robat-i-Paskaran.

Mellaart (1965 *b*: 130-31) indicates that the Badakhshan region holds not only the lapis source, but also sources for steatite, diorite, serpentine, carnelian, and hematite. Ghirshman (1954: 26) mentions that carnelian may be mined in Iran but gives no exact location.

Iron oxides, which were used for pigments, are known for the western foothills near Konya in Central Anatolia (Mellaart, 1967: 217) and from Hormuz Island at the entrance to the Persian Gulf (Cressey, 1960: 514). Hole and Flannery (1968: 181) indicate that there is a specular hematite source in Fars in southwestern Iran, and Wertime (1968) has written that iron ores are known from northern Fars into southern Kirman province. Hematite of intermediate quality has been located in the Negev where the Nahal Param issues into the Arava Valley (Orni and Efrat, 1964: 286).

Our recent studies here at the University of Michigan on magnetite and hematite from Oaxaca clearly show that different iron oxide sources may be distinguished by elemental analysis. The above list of localities for iron products certainly does not exhaust the number of occurrences of the material. It would be worthwhile to test known sources against archaeological occurrences to form some idea of the use and movement of iron oxides in the Near East.

There are two known source areas of turquoise. One is located near Meshed in northeastern Iran (Cressey, 1960: 514). This is presumably the major Near Eastern source. There are also turquoise sources in the Negev and in Sinai (Anati, 1963: 42; 1962: 29).

Alabaster is said to occur near Kayseri between Nevşehir and Erciyas Dağ (Mellaart, 1967; J. Kolars, personal communication). Burney (1964: 56) suggests that there is an alabaster source close to Yanik Tepe, near Tabriz, "especially since it was so lavishly used for the dado of the Blue Mosque in Tabriz." Tobler (1950: 200), in dealing with the alabaster (and steatite and serpentine) at Tepe Gawra comments that sources are found in Iran. Lloyd and Safar (1945: 285) state, however, that alabaster, heavily impregnated with sulfur, may be found in the Fatha (Tigris) Gorge, approximately 110 km. south of Shura, Iraq.

In the regions around Mosul there are quarries of basalt, limestone, and soft gray-and-white or green-and-white marble (known locally as Mosul Marble) (Tobler, 1950: 200). The Mosul-Kirkuk region is also a well-known source area for natural seeps of bitumen (Cressey, 1960: 194). Chemical studies of bitumen are currently being undertaken by Dr. R. Marschner of the American Oil Company in order to learn the composition, origin, and processing of this material (H. T. Wright, personal communication). From a study of bitumen from Sakheri Sughir, an Early Dynastic village in southern alluvial Mesopotamia, H. T. Wright (in press) suggests that "bitumen was distributed in small solid cakes and heated when needed for use." Bitumen is also found in lumps or masses on the surface of the Dead Sea and along its shore (Anati, 1962: 30). Dolomite is known south of Mosul near Fatha Gorge (Lloyd and Safar, (1945: 285).

"Greenstone" was a popular material for celts during the Neolithic at Çatal Hüyük and in Cyro-Cilicia. According to Mellaart, there are two greenstone sources just west of Hacilar and one southwest of Çatal Hüyük on a low ridge between Cumra and Karaman. Cinnabar, used for pigments at Çatal Hüyük, was mined near Sizma, northwest of Konya, which is the area of the Çukurkent group sites. The white marble at Çatal Hüyük is said to be available in Western Anatolia (Mellaart, 1967: 212).

Perhaps the most exciting recent work in the Near East is Wertime's investigations into the problems of early metallurgy. Copper was used as early as 7000 B.C. at Çayönü. It is known in the Ali Kosh phase in the Deh Luran and at Suberde by the mid-seventh millennium B.C., and at Çatal Hüyük in Level IX (C-14 date of 6240 ± 99 B.C., P-779). At the latter site, lead beads also appear in Level IX (Mellaart, 1967: 217).

There are a large number of copper and lead mines in the Near East and many of them, particularly in Iran, have been mentioned by Wertime (1968). Both metals occur near Maden in southeastern Turkey; historically this source, located very near Çayönü, has been an extremely important copper producer. By the fifth millennium B.C., copper was being smelted at the site of Timra in the Negev. Wertime has surveyed and recorded an impressive number of copper sources in Iran. Important fifth millennium B.C. sites like Tal-i-Iblis have produced crucibles used in smelting (Caldwell and Shahmirzadi, 1966). Excavations at Sialk yielded copper artifacts.

Although many "sources" of raw materials are known in the Near East, in many cases it is impossible at this time to name the exact mine which produced a certain artifact. In contrast to obsidian where we are on firm ground, we can only suggest probable directions in which goods were moving. Thus, while it is fairly certain that the copper at Çayönü came from the Maden mine, did the Çatal Hüyük and Suberde copper derive from this same source or from a more local source? This type of question is still a major problem to be solved in the Near East.

THE PRECERAMIC: 7500 TO 6250 B.C.

The movement of nonlocal goods begins prior to the time period under consideration here. Obsidian appears in the Zagros and at Mureybat before 7500 B.C. About a dozen *Dentalium* shell beads and two large scallop shells were recovered in the Zarzian levels at Pa Sangar Rockshelter in Khorramabad by Hole and Flannery (1968: 160). They have not yet been identified as to species and their source is unknown. *Dentalium* shells also appear in the Natufian of Palestine, with both Mediterranean and Red Sea species being recovered at Hayonium Cave in Western Galilee (Bar-Yosef and Tchernov, 1966: 137). Again, the shells were fashioned into ornaments (cf. also the use of *Dentalium* at El Wad).

One of the earliest sites to show more extensive trade relations is Pre-Pottery Neolithic Jericho. In the preceramic levels three nonlocal materials have been recovered: (*a*) Central Anatolian obsidian, (*b*) turquoise matrix in lumps from the Sinai, and (*c*) cowrie shells from the Mediterranean (Anati, 1962: 29).

Jericho is situated near the Dead Sea, which was a source for three items of some value during historic times: salt, bitumen, and sulfur. Historically, the Dead Sea was the major salt source for the surrounding area: "Remains of salt mines on the shores of the Dead Sea are very common, and these salt mines are frequently mentioned in the Bible" (Anati, 1963: 248). The Bedouin, in historic times, are known to have constructed artificial evaporation lagoons on the shore of the Dead Sea and then to have transported the salt to markets in Jerusalem, Hebron, Beersheba, and Gaza (Anati, 1963: 249).

Bitumen occurs as lumps on the surface of the Dead Sea. It was employed as a cement and its utilization extends from historic times back to the Natufian in this area. It is used by the Judean Talamirah Bedouin for moulding into vessels and in Bethlehem and Jerusalem for fashioning handicraft items like crosses, rosaries, and arabesque bowls (Anati, 1962: 31).

Sulfur may be collected on the shore of the Dead Sea or in the plains near Jericho. The Bedouin utilized sulfur for preparing medicines and for lighting fires, and blocks of sulfur have been recovered in the pre-pottery levels at Jericho (Anati, 1963: 250).

After considering the "public works" of Jericho and the subsistence potential of the immediate area, Anati (1963: 248) has decided that only "trade could have been the main source of wealth and power at Jericho." He feels that "incipient" agriculture, hunting, and fishing could not have produced "the enormous surplus suggested by the gigantic public structures of Jericho" (1963: 247), and suggests that only trade, and in particular the salt trade, could have provided the people at Jericho "with the greater part of the surplus indicated by the archaeological excavations" (p. 249).

There seem to be some problems with Anati's interpretations of Jericho. First of all, he significantly underplays the role of agriculture, or at least the opportunity for collecting wild grains in the Jordan Valley. There is evidence now in the form of domesticated grains to indicate that agriculture was being practiced during Pre-Pottery Neolithic times at Jericho (Flannery, personal communication). Harlan and Zohary (1966), in addition, have pointed out the extensive stands of wild wheat in the Jordan Valley and the high probability that wheat domestication began in this area. Thus, a high productivity of cereal grains is indicated.

Second, were these three raw materials important enough commodities that their trade alone would have supported a population the size of Pre-Pottery Neolithic Jericho? Were salt, bitumen, and sulfur so desired that they were widely traded not only to the local Jordan Valley villages, but also to the Anatolian Plateau from where the Jericho obsidian was obtained? Although many investigators believe that the salt trade was a major factor in the rise of the Hallstatt culture of Europe around the sixth century B.C. (Piggott, 1965), there are no data to suggest that salt was traded from Jericho to the Anatolian Plateau, where local sources (e.g. Tuz Gölü) were readily available. Also, the recovery of sulfur at Jericho does not indicate that it, too, was being sent out of the Jordan Valley to the Anatolian Plateau or the Zagros-Taurus arc. Thus, the long distance trade was certainly very minor in nature.

Even so, the indications that Jericho was participating in trade networks is apparent: the similarities in certain artifact styles (e.g. compare the ancestor skulls at contemporary Aceramic Hacilar) and the Central Anatolian obsidian attest to this. But to attribute to long distance trade the major reason for Jericho's florescence is to ignore Jericho's favorable location at an oasis spring. Further, the economic potential provided by the wild grains and the early agriculture should have been particularly high.

These latter two points may, indeed, be coupled with trade. Yet, I fail to see in Anati's analysis any evidence to suggest that the long distance trade served as the main source of wealth. In contrast, Jericho seems to have served as a regional economic center, with villages like Munhata and Beisamoun lying in the hinter lands. If one may project the Bedouin's role back 8500-9000 years (and this is a risky assumption), nomadic peoples may have collected salt, etc., from the Dead Sea and carried it to Jericho for trade. People from the smaller Jordan Valley villages might have exchanged goods (e.g., there is a gypsum source c. 1.0 km. from Manhata) at Jericho.

Thus, one may see two trade systems at work in the Jordan Valley. The first involves the trade of local resources such as salt. These materials were possibly collected by groups similar to the Bedouin, or perhaps by hunters-and-gatherers. The goods were brought into Jericho and then exchanged with villagers from the smaller Jordan Valley settlements. The second system concerns long distance trade. The material from this trade accumulated primarily at Jericho. For example, for the Pre-Pottery Neolithic, there are over 400 pieces of obsidian from Jericho. There is one piece of obsidian from the PPNB at Munhata, and only four obsidian specimens are currently known from Beisamoun. Both cowrie shells and turquoise are absent at Munhata; they are present at Jericho.

Even though the long distance trade did not provide much in the way of quantity in raw materials to the smaller Jordan Valley villages, it was economically significant in other respects. A major animal in the diet at PPNB Munhata was "wild" sheep, and wild sheep are not native to this area but are native to the Zagros (Flannery, personal communication). We know from the group 4c obsidian at Beidha, Beisamoun, and Ramad that the Van region and Palestine were in contact. Thus, the long distance trade served as a vehicle by which sheep were brought into the Jordan Valley prior to 6500 B.C. At the same time, domesticated wheat was moved from Palestine into the Zagros-Taurus arc as outlined above.

In the preceramic phases of the early villages in the Zagros-Taurus area, there is evidence that the long distance trade in obsidian and shells, which was seen in the Zarzian, continued. In the Bus Mordeh phase in the Deh Luran, "we have in the presence of obsidian and cowrie shells, limited but positive evidence of trade" (Hole, 1968: 256). Long distance trade is seen in the form of obsidian in the Ali Kosh phase. In addition new raw materials appear: turquoise and copper which were made into beads, and red ochre.

Hole and Flannery (1968: 177) suggest that the turquoise may be from the mines near Meshed in Iran. It is interesting to note, however, that the only contemporary site with turquoise is Jericho, which is said by Anati (1963) to have derived from the Sinai. As domesticated wheat is known from the Deh Luran as early as the Bus Mordeh phase, it would be of considerable interest to have

60 OBSIDIAN ANALYSES AND PREHISTORIC TRADE

petrological and/or elemental analyses of the turquoise from both sites.

The same applies to the copper. It is known at this early date only at Çayönü (c. 7000 B.C.), Suberde (c. 6500 B.C.) and at Çatal Hüyük beginning in Level IX (c. 6240 B.C.). There is a major copper source about 20 km. from Çayönü (the Maden mines). It would, again, be useful to test these specimens, since groups 1g and 4c obsidian are found at both Çayönü and Ali Kosh.

Flannery (1965) has presented a model for subsistence during the late hunting-and-gathering and preceramic Neolithic stages in the Zagros. He sees in the former stage, bands migrating seasonally through the four major ecological zones (the high plateau, the oak-pistachio uplands, the Assyrian steppe, and alluvial Mesopotamia). Presumably, each band's territory would have included a portion of each major ecological zone. Thus, each band would have had access to all the major food resouces and local food trade between bands would have been rare or absent. Midden debris, however, does indicate that the inhabitants of the early settled villages in the Zagros ate the same foods, in about the same quantities, as did the early post-Pleistocene hunters-and-gatherers (Flannery, 1968a).

There are three possibilities to consider. For local trade, a major change might have occurred when migratory hunting bands settled into permanent agricultural villages, but continued through local food exchanges to utilize food resources specific to the other ecological zones. Rather than the movement of people, foodstuffs were traded across ecological boundaries.

There is a second new adaptive pattern which began during the preceramic phases. Hole (1968) suggests that by the Bus Mordeh phase villagers were seasonally moving herds into the mountain pastures. This does not mean that nomadism as an economic specialty was being practiced, but this is a mechanism, separate from trade, by which the former ecological zones were still being exploited by the newly settled agriculturalists. This might, then, be an alternate explanation as to why the midden debris from the early village sites is similar to that of the sites of the earlier hunting period. The movement of shepherds into the mountains is also seen by Hole (1968: 257) as a vehicle by which some of the long distance trade (particularly in obsidian) was carried on: "If we seek a mechanism for ensuring continuous trade, we can probably find it in the seasonal gathering of shepherds in mountain valleys along the route where most of the obsidian seems to have been distributed."

A third possibility is that hunting bands continued to occupy areas not yet inhabited by agriculturalists. They too then, might have entered into some kind of trade relations with the villagers. Here, the model of the early historic trading patterns of the western Great Lakes comes to mind (Wright, 1967).

In considering trade at this time period Renfrew, Dixon and Cann (1966) suggest that ceremonial gift exchange does not apply here as the mechanism, seemingly due to a misunderstanding of what ceremonial gift exchange involves. "Obsidian was generally traded as an unworked raw material rather than in the form of attractively finished objects" (Renfrew *et al.*, 1966: 51). Discussions of ceremonial gift exchange (e.g. Berndt, 1951; Harding, 1967; Stanner, 1933-34) indicate, however, that raw materials as well as finished products are moved by this mechanism.

Renfrew, Dixon and Cann (1966: 51) also suggest that silent trade is a too "sophisticated mode of exchange" to be applicable. The discussion of silent trade by Price (1967) shows clearly that this mechanism involves exchange between cultural groups of distinctly different levels of social complexity (e.g., State-Tribe). Thus, I would agree with Renfrew and his associates (1966) that silent trade does not apply, but for different reasons.

In summary, trade during the preceramic is significant because it was during this time that settled village life began, and plants and animals were domesticated. Flannery (1965) in his discussion of origins of domestication has emphasized that the important feature in plant domestication is the transmission of the wild grains out of their natural habitat. It seems that the developing long distance trade, particularly in obsidian, played a significant role in providing both the routes and the contacts for the movement of grains into new ecological habitats.

Obsidian from Lake Van reached the Deh Luran by the Bus Mordeh phase, is known along the middle reaches of the Euphrates in the preceramic, and entered the southern Levant by the PPNB. Central Anatolian obsidian has been recovered as far south as Beidha and occurred at Jericho, Munhata 6, and Beisamoun in the Jordan Valley. If, as seems likely from the work of Harlan and Zohary (1966), the modern domesticated wheat derives from the Jordan Valley race, then the obsidian trade indicates routes by which this grain may have been transported into new ecological zones in Central Anatolia and the Zagros-Taurus arc.

Beginning with the Karim Shahir phase in the Zagros, all of the sites in the early stages of settled village life had a few pieces of obsidian. Thus, by 7500 B.C. this raw material was known throughout the Zagros-Taurus arc. By the end of the preceramic in this area, the usual count in quantity per site is, conservatively, more than 300 pieces. Thus, by the time that domesticated wheat moved into the Lake Van obsidian source area, the routes for its dispersal throughout the Zagros were already established by the earlier obsidian trade.

The abundance of "wild" sheep in PPNB levels in the Jordan Valley (which is not a natural habitat zone for this animal) is suggestive of further contacts between the Zagros-Taurus arc and the Levant. It appears evident that sheep initially moved against wheat and followed the same route being utilized for obsidian.

THE EARLY CERAMIC PHASES: 6250 TO 5200 B.C.

In the Zagros-Taurus arc, this time range saw a number of innovations and improvements in subsistence techniques and artifacts. Ceramics appear toward the beginning of the period and by the Sabz phase in the Deh Luran, there is evidence of both irrigation agriculture and cattle domestication. Farther to the west, domesticated cattle are known from Çatal Hüyük at about 6000 B.C. (Flannery, personal communication).

Settlement pattern surveys from the Zagros give evidence of fully settled villages in the lower elevations of the valleys and small camps in the higher elevations which appear to have been used seasonally by herders. Tepe Guran, for example, showed evidence of substantial houses and year-round occupations, while nearby (but higher) Sarab exhibited neither. Hole (1968: 255) describes Sarab as follows: "It appears to have been a camp used seasonally by herders whose parent village, if any, might well have been like Guran or Ali Kosh." In the caves of Khorramabad, Deh Luran type ceramics have been recovered. These shepherd camps suggest a pattern of transhumant nomadism to Hole. By the Mohammad Jaffar and temporally related phases, then, there seems to be a trend toward economic specialization of groups within the valley system, and in the areas of higher elevation in the Zagros transhumant herding was becoming more important than farming (Hole, 1968).

At Ali Kosh, in the Bus Mordeh and Ali Kosh phases, goats outnumber sheep about 150 to 1 (Flannery, personal communication). In the Mohammad Jaffar phase the trend is reversed and in the later periods sheep come to outnumber goats as the most common domesticated animal. This is the early historic pattern. In terms of trade, it appears that local exchange of meat and hides for grain began during the early sixth millennium B.C. in the Zagros.

Barth (1964) has discussed the nomadic Basseri of Fars Province, southwestern Iran, in some detail. He has pointed out the dependency of these nomads on the agricultural villages for flour, fruits, vegetables, etc. Other goods like material for clothes, jewelry, and ceramics are also obtained by trade. The products exchanged by the Basseri are almost exclusively clarified butter, wool, lambskins, and livestock.

Today, the bulk of this trade takes place in the town markets, however, there is no evidence for market structures in the Zagros during the sixth millennium B.C. Thus, a different exchange mechanism was operating. It seems likely that the early stages of herding involved local villagers taking flocks into the mountain pastures during the summer and returning to the parent village for the winter. As various groups left the village and began full-time specialization in sheep and goat herding, the exchanges probably took place along surviving kinship lines with the village.

A study of stylistic elements in artifact types such as ceramics might show clear relationships between one or more nomad encampments and a contemporary agricultural village. This might then suggest direct economic and kinship ties between herders and one central village. However, where such stylistic linkages are found to connect a nomad encampment with villages from several valley systems, economic but not kinship ties might be indicated.

Clearly, one may also look to the nomads as a mechanism for the movement of long distance trade goods. As Hole (1968: 258) has phrased it for the Zagros region: "There is no reason to think that any of these items [e.g. obsidian] could not have been procured through exchange by shepherds coming in contact seasonally with other people."

At Matarrah, a wide variety of materials was utilized for the groundstone industry including limestone, diabase, dolerite, and metamorphic schist for the larger tools. About 40 beads were described by the authors, most of which came from the upper phase. The most common materials for the beads were limestone, carnelian, marble, chalcedony, and soapstone. Marble was also utilized for "nails" and a flat, polished semicircular ornament. There is one bead identified as probably being turquoise (see Braidwood *et al.*, 1952).

Paint pigments and metals from the excavations at Hassuna were submitted for chemical analysis. The pigments were all natural iron oxides. The metals also included a lump of galena from Level Ia (the lowest) and copper carbonate (malachite). The authors (Lloyd and Safar, 1945: 286) suggest that the Fatha (Tigris) Gorge, approximately 110 km. south of Shura is the iron oxide source (this is also a bitumen source area) and the Tuz Khurmatu district, about 100 km. from Shura, is suggested as the copper source.

A number of beads, amulets, pendants, and other ornaments were recovered at Hassuna. Raw materials for these items include turquoise, limestone, greenstone, amethyst (?), diorite, obsidian, and possibly malachite.

To the north, the site of Yanik Tepe, near Tabriz, is of some interest. This site was occupied first during the first half of the sixth millennium B.C. (Burney, 1964). It was a fairly substantial settlement of mud brick houses, with gypsum plaster used on some floors and walls. Alabaster was found to be utilized for bowls and loom weights as well as for bracelets which Burney (1964) compares with the limestone bracelets from Sarab. As noted above, Burney has suggested that the alabaster source is local. During the second half of this millennium, and later, alabaster was a common raw material for ornaments in sites in northern Mesopotamia.

One of these sites is Tell es-Sawwan. Here, alabaster was utilized for tiny dishes, plates, bowls, cups, flasks, large pots, beads, "phallic symbols," and a series of mother goddess figurines. Some of the latter had bitumen caps and eyes inlaid with shell (El-Wailly and Abu es-Soof, 1965: 22). Other imported raw materials include carnelian and *Dentalium* shells, as well as copper beads and obsidian.

The site is an agricultural village on the middle Tigris, and the Samarran ceramics clearly link it with the type site of Samarra located some 11 km. upriver. Artifacts from certain houses suggest they were residences of people of higher status, because a large portion of the alabaster came from Building I in Level I. There also appear to be clear differences in burial goods, again, suggesting higher status individuals.

It seems evident, then, that certain raw materials were not being redistributed, but were being channeled to specific households or individuals. This is one of the earliest examples of accumulation rather than redistribution in Greater Mesopotamia, and sets the stage for later developments.

From the artifacts and sites discussed above, it seems clear that local trade became of greater economic importance early in this time period in the Zagros. Long distance trade for the procurement of raw materials grew slowly, both in quantity and in the addition of new goods like alabaster, marble, etc. Evidence of status differentiation is not seen in any marked degree until the Hassuna phase and, in a more restricted sense, to Late Hassuna. One of the earliest sites to strongly exhibit this feature is Tell es-Sawwan. In contrast, in Central Anatolia, the site of Çatal Hüyük appears to show possible social stratification at a somewhat earlier date.

The entire occupation of Çatal Hüyük is contained within this time span (by C-14 dates, from 6300 to 5500 B.C.)[1] This site is viewed as an "enigma" by many archaeologists. The excavator has used the term "urban" to describe the site and has spoken of "religious specialists" who "did not bother to weave their own cloth or chip their own tools" but "went to the bazaar and utilized the handiwork of others." "The objects found in the houses and shrines of the quarter are all finished products, and the area of the workshops where these items were made, sold or bartered, must lie elsewhere on the mound" (Mellaart, 1967: 211). With these hypothesized shrines and technological and religious specializations, Mellaart has presented a site to us which is some 1000 to 1500 years ahead of developments in Mesopotamia.

Trade is certainly indicated by the use of a variety of raw materials: copper, iron oxides, obsidian, marble, cinnabar, alabaster, wood (e.g. fir from the Taurus), limestone, greenstone, and Mediterranean shells. The area circumscribed by what Mellaart (1967: 28-29) calls the "Çatal Hüyük Early Neolithic" contains most of the sources for these raw materials. He has suggested that control of the obsidian trade was one source of wealth for the site and that the Hasan Dağ, was a major source. Without samples from this flow, this can not be established; but it is worthwhile to note that all of the specimens from Çatal Hüyük tested by Renfrew, Dixon and Cann (1966) belong to group 1e-f (Acigöl Locality 3). Although it is about 225 km. to this source from the site, the flow lies on the northeastern edge of the Çatal Hüyük Early Neolithic zone.

The probable alabaster source is also located in the same general region, slightly to the east of Acigöl between Nevşehir and

---

[1] The half-life of 5570 years is used for all C-14 dates in this paper.

Erciyes Dağ. A major salt source is found near the site of Ilicapinar along the northern edge of the zone. This site has a Çatal Hüyük-like obsidian industry (Mellaart, 1958). To the west, copper and cinnabar may be recovered near the Çukurkent group of sites. Greenstone is known approximately 60 km. to the southeast of the site on a low ridge between Cumra and Karaman. To the south and west of the Konya Plain, limestone, wood, and iron oxides are available in the Taurus. Iron oxides also occur in the western hills behind Konya, and Mellaart says marble is present in Western Anatolia (1967: 212).

Çatal Hüyük is the largest (32 acres) of a series of sites on the Central Anatolian Plateau within the Çatal Hüyük Early Neolithic zone. Like Tell es-Sawwan, the occupation of this site is an early manifestation of the permanent settlement of a new ecological zone. As noted above, it is situated within easy access of a number of major raw materials, and is located between the major Neolithic centers: the Balkans, the Levant, and northern Mesopotamia. The former region is important in that cattle were apparently first domesticated here (Flannery, personal communication) and spread to Çatal Hüyük by around 6000 B.C. and to the Deh Luran by the Sabz phase.

The internal structure of the site is not yet well known. The "residential" and "bazaar centers," in contradistinction to the "religious quarter," are still to be demonstrated. We still do not know if goods were manufactured on the site or were carried in from the source areas in finished condition. What does seem to be clear, however, is that Çatal Hüyük was a major regional center.

Many of the products recovered on this site are known outside this area. For example, greenstone celts and obsidian are common in Syro-Cilicia (e.g., at Mersin). Although Bialor (1962) denies it, there are clear resemblances between the lithic assemblages of the two regions. At Mersin, greenstone celts are known in Levels XXVIII-XXIV, marble beads in XXVI-XXV, alabaster in XXVII-XXIV, and obsidian from Basal Mersin through Level XX as outlined above. A second nonlocal product at Mersin is prase, a silica mineral, which has two possible sources both 400 miles away: along the Bosphorus and in the Sinai (Garstang, 1953: 72).

In the Amuq Phase A, greenstone was utilized for vessels, stamp seals, and a single pendant; it apparently was not used for celts. In Phase B and the First Mixed Range, the same artifacts were fashioned of this material. In these latter phases, carnelian and marble were also utilized, and in the First Mixed Range there were 49 obsidian beads. In Phase B, there was a worked stone with metal adhering to it; however, the investigators comment that the object was apparently not catalogued and never reached Chicago. In the First Mixed Range, there were two copper reamers and a piece of wirelike lead (Braidwood and Braidwood, 1960).

There are certainly clear links between Central Anatolia and Syro-Cilicia in the form of Central Anatolian obsidian. If the prase at Mersin is the Bosphorus variety, there is a second possible link although this material is not reported from contemporary sites in Central Anatolia. In this vein, it would be extremely interesting to have analyses of the greenstone, copper, and alabaster. For example, is the variety of alabaster used at Mersin the same as that utilized at Çatal Hüyük or is it similar to the es-Sawwan type?

One may point out that there is much to be learned about the movement of goods in Syro-Cilicia and Central Anatolia. Mersin's position near the Cilician Gates suggests a closer contact with Central Anatolia than with northern Mesopotamia. This is confirmed by the Central Anatolian obsidian at Mersin. The part played by Çatal Hüyük in the long distance trade with Syro-Cilicia is still to be determined. That Çatal Hüyük was a focus for local trade within the Çatal Hüyük Early Neolithic zone seems evident from the large amount of goods recovered on the site. If manufacturing centers are found on the site, in separate quarters, this may argue for specialized traders who transported goods off the Plateau. This is still to be demonstrated, however, in the excavations.

HALAF - UBAID

Shortly before 5000 B.C., the first large settlement appeared at Eridu in southern alluvial Mesopotamia. In the north, the sites of Chagar Bazar, Arpachiyah, Nineveh, and, at about 5000 B.C., Tepe Gawra, were also first occupied. From this time period, temples and village specialization are now evident in the archaeological record. Status differentiation and ranking became more marked. It is also possible that town markets were functioning.

The settlement pattern of Mesopotamia may be summarized briefly before discussing trade mechanics. There appear to be five types of settlements: (a) town and temple centers (e.g., Gawra and Eridu); (b) small irrigation farming villages lacking temples (e.g., Ras as-Amiya); (c) permanent villages oriented around dry farming (Hole and Flannery, 1968: 182); (d) pastoral camps in caves (e.g., Kunji Cave); and (e) craft speciality villages (e.g., Tal-i-Iblis).

The local economics of this time period are still poorly known. The transformation to irrigation agriculture had taken place during the Sabz phase in southwestern Iran and was now being practiced by breaching the natural levees of the bifurcating channels of the lower Euphrates (Adams, 1966). During the fifth millennium B.C., the basic barley and sheep economy of the early civilizations of alluvial Mesopotamia and Khuzistan had been formed. Domesticated cattle were also of some importance at Eridu and Ras al'Amiya during the Ubaid phase; at the latter site they make up 45 per cent of the faunal remains (Hole and Flannery, 1968: 192, 197). Large quantities of fish bone in the Late Ubaid temple debris at Eridu indicate that fishing was an important occupation (Adams, 1966: 50). Further, as the inhabitants of the southern alluvial valley lacked direct access to many natural resources, these products had to be gained through long distance trade.

From a later time period, Early Dynastic texts indicate that four specialized subsistence zones were utilized in the southern alluvium: 1) field cultivation along the levee back slopes and the margins of the swamps; 2) garden and orchard cultivation in the low-lying areas adjacent to the swamps; 3) herding in the fallow fields; and 4) fishing and utilization of the swamps and rivers. "The important point about these subsistence alternatives is that they were pursued by specialists in whose activities and interrelations the formal organizations of the community played a substantial and intervening role" (Adams, 1966: 48). The local movement of goods within the society was not through trade but was accomplished by a redistributive network which had its focus in the dominant temple or palace (p. 51).

How does this model apply to the southern alluvial valley at the earlier time period under consideration here? I suspect, and this is still to be demonstrated, that the new adaptation, focused around the temple, was established early in the settlement by permanent villages of the southern alluvium. The substantial offering of fish in the Late Ubaid temple at Eridu recalls the Early Dynastic pattern. The temples at Eridu date back at least to Level XVIII (c. 5200 B.C.). The earliest temples had kilns associated with them. High status burials of men, women, and children in brick tombs had nonutilitarian pottery as grave goods (Lloyd, 1948), presumably from these temple kilns.

The movement into a new ecological zone, the possibility of subsistence specialists, and the high status burials suggesting inherited status bring to mind Fried's (1967: 185-226) concept of "stratified society." If these surmises are correct, we are not dealing with local trade here but redistribution through the temple. Long distance trade did occur and will be discussed below.

In the northern Khuzistan steppe, the chief grains were wheat and barley, which were grown both by dry farming and irrigation. The herding of sheep and goats was practiced, and cattle supplemented the faunal list. In Luristan and Kurdistan, the main crop was wheat which was grown by dry farming. Sheep and goat herding was also of considerable importance and was supplemented by pigs, cattle, and barley (Hole and Flannery, 1968: 194).

Although a substantial number of large sites has been excavated in the middle and upper reaches of the Tigris and Euphrates, we know little of local economics. In the historic period according to Babylonian texts, the Chagar Bazar area was an important grain center for barley (Gadd, 1937: 93). By the Halaf period at Arpachiyah in Level VII there are found the Developed Tholoi: a group of buildings whose function is not clearly understood. Some specialization is evident at Arpachiyah where a potter and stone-worker's shop was excavated in TT 6 (Mallowan and Rose, 1935: 105). Temples are definitely known from the Ubaid period at Tepe Gawra, as well as burials showing different qualities and quantities of grave goods (Tobler, 1950). Actual evidence of stratification is difficult to arrive at here because of the lack of age and sex data, even though the burial goods are well described. Because of the lack of data, however, I am hesitant about extending the redistributive model to cover the Mosul area.

There is evidence, though, of nomad encampments, particularly in caves (e.g., Kunji Cave in Luristan, Diyan and Bastoon in the Baradost Mountains, and a cave near Sakçe Gözü) (Hole and Flannery, 1968: 182; Lines, n.d.: 114, 137). Shepherds still frequent caves today, often building huts or pens with dry laid stone walls like those found in Kunji Cave (Hole and Flannery, 1968: 182). Each of these caves, as well as more recently discovered ones in western Iran have Ubaid ceramics, (Flannery, personal communication), and often earlier and later ceramic types suggesting seasonal occupation over a considerable time period. There seems to be little doubt as to the existence of full-time nomadism by the Ubaid phase, and thus an active trade of meat and animal products in the towns and villages for craft goods and foodstuffs not raised nor manufactured by nomadic peoples.

One may discuss long distance trade and the movement into areas of nonlocal raw materials with somewhat more ease. With the new social stratification, there appears in the archaeological record of the Near East an increasing use of nonlocal materials for articles not directly related to subsistence. Not only do new raw materials become utilized, but others, like obsidian, are used in new forms and new contexts. Obsidian was not only fashioned into tools by the late Halafian period, but bowls, beads, stamps, etc., were also manufactured of this material. Many of these new raw materials are recovered primarily in burial contexts or within the confines of a single house or a single room.

In northern Greater Mesopotamia the list of raw materials used for making vases, beads, and other ornaments is impressive. At Arpachiyah obsidian, black steatite, glazed white steatite, limestone, carnelian, calcite, quartz, frit, shell, serpentine, lapis lazuli, and small *Dentalium* shells were used (Mallowan and Rose, 1935). The same raw materials were also utilized at Chagar Bazar (Mallowan, 1936; 1937) and at Tepe Gawra (Tobler, 1950). At the latter site, particularly during the late Ubaid, these materials were used extensively for seals; in fact most of the Gawra stamp seals are of stone. As Tobler has pointed out: "most of the varieties of stone used in the manufacture of seals (such as steatite, serpentine, lapis lazuli, agate, carnelian, hematite, and obsidian) are not found in a native state in Mesopotamia and must have been imported from some distant source" (p. 176). Lapis is also known at Nineveh 2 (Late Ubaid) (Hermann, 1968: 29), but in the south, lapis does not appear until Jemdat Nasr times.

Other imported materials also appear. The Persian Gulf shell *Cyraea vitellus* is known from Level 7-8 at Chagar Bazar (Mallowan, 1936: 10, note 4). Persian Gulf shells are also known from Sialk II.

The use of metal tools and ornaments becomes widespread during this time span. At Arpachiyah, a conical piece of lead was recovered in the burnt house in TT 6 (Climax Halaf) (Mallowan and Rose, 1935: 104). Also from this site were two fragments of copper pins and a chisel with a slightly splayed end cast in an open mold. A single copper bead was found in Level 12 (Halaf) at Chagar Bazar (Mallowan, 1936: 10). At Tepe Gawra, Level XVII produced a copper ring and chisel, Level XIII an awl, and in Level XII (the end of Ubaid) copper implements became important and the first gold beads appeared. Lines (n.d. 178) states that "the greater number of seals in Gawra XIII may reflect an increased use of metal tools at this point."

In Phase F of the Amuq sequence at Judaidah, Braidwood and Braidwood (1960: 245, Fig. 185) recovered seven reamers of a copper-nickel alloy, two copper chisels (one copper-nickel-aluminum-calcium-iron-silicon), one pin, one blade, and one point of copper-nickel. Copper awls occur in an Ubaid context (Level IVc) at Sakçe Gözü (Taylor et al., 1950: 123, Fig. 33, No. 4). Copper pins first appear in Levels XXII and XXI at Mersin and also at Mersin there is a copper chisel and a stamp seal in Level XVII, 6 roll beaded pins and 2 axes in Level XVI, 2 molded copper chisels in XV_B, and 2 long copper needles in Levels XIV-XIII in Room 163 (Garstang, 1953: 167).

Lines (n.d.) has outlined the use of copper in some Iranian sites contemporary with Ubaid. Copper is known from the upper levels of Tepe Jaffarabad. In Susa A (Ubaid 4) there is a full use of copper in the form of axes, chisels, pins, and mirrors (Le Breton, 1957: 93). At the end of Sialk I there are copper pins and awls (?), in Sialk II copper awls, and slightly later in Sialk III $_{4-5}$ cast copper. In Giyan V-B there are copper pins and in V-C a copper chisel. The chisels from Arpachiyah, Tepe Gawra, Susa A, and Giyan V-C are all of the casted variety with a slightly splayed end called Susa Type 1 by Lines (n.d.: 178). Pins similar to those at Sialk III were recovered in the Mehmeh phase (4500-4100 B.C.) at Tepe Sabz (Hole and Flannery, 1968: 191). The earliest Bakun A levels produced copper objects, including a seal in Level 1 (Lines, n.d.). There is a twisted piece of gold wire from an Ubaid context at Ur. Other fifth millennium B.C. sites showing metal include Chesmeh Ali, Tepe Hissar, Tepe Anau, and Tepe Yarin (Wertime, 1968: 927).

When Lines (n.d.: 219) wrote her Ubaid synthesis, she noted that although there were abundant data indicating use of metal during the Ubaid, there was no evidence of craft production of metallurgy at any Ubaid site. Evidence is now available at the contemporary site of Tal-i-Iblis where the smelting of copper ores is attested prior to 4000 B.C. (Caldwell and Shahmirzadi, 1966; Wertime, 1968). Along with Tal-i-Iblis, there are a number of sites situated adjacent or near to the copper, iron oxide, etc., sources which rim the central Persian Desert (Wertime, 1968).

In this connection it may be noted that there is evidence of a number of specialized villages. Besides Tal-i-Iblis and the Iranian copper-producing sites, Tilki Tepe appears to have specialized in the preparation of obsidian for trade, and in Persian Kurdistan, Murian for flint production (Braidwood, 1960; Flannery, personal communication). Although the Murian area flint is of a poorer quality, it had replaced the more local and better quality flint used in the Deh Luran by the Sabz phase (Hole and Flannery, 1968: 185).

Burton-Brown (1962: 31) has commented that "it is curious that in most Near Eastern sites virtually no kilns have been found." Besides at Eridu, they have been found also at Burton-Brown's site of Kara Tepe in Shahriyar Province, Iran. Ceramics from this site suggest it is contemporaneous with the Mehmeh phase in the Deh Luran (Flannery, personal communication). One of the more spectacular finds is the Yunus Kilns at Carchemish where the remains of 15 kilns were recovered in an area of 3 by 6 m. Found scattered among the kilns were slate palettes, pounders and grinders for working clay and pigments, celts, and a bone graver. There were also a number of discarded pots, which, according to Woolley (1934: 151), were imperfect in some manner. This occupation (Halafian) has been interpreted as one specializing in the production of ceramics.

There are also suggestions of craftsmen in single villages. At Arpachiyah in the burnt house in TT 6, lumps of red ochre and palettes were recovered next to painted pots. The house was located adjacent to kilns in the center of the site and the inhabitant appears to have been a potter. In this same house, the obsidian vase mentioned earlier was recovered along with vases of other types of stone, amulets, jewelry, figurines, and obsidian tools and cores. The investigators suggest that one room was also occupied by a stone worker (Mallowan and Rose, 1935: 105).

There are two major points to be made in connection with the long distance trade of raw materials. One is the spread of ceramic and other stylistic features over wide areas in a very short time. The spread of the southern Ubaid into Northern Mesopotamia during Ubaid 3 (c. 4300 B.C.) is an excellent example. The second point is the concentration of exotic raw materials and products in the large sites, beginning predominantly in the Ubaid but existing in Mesopotamia on a smaller scale by late Hassuna times. This occurred particularly in situations suggesting unequal access to these goods: that is, as symbols of status differentiation.

The first of these points is often explained by recourse to migration theories. For example, the spread of Ubaid is often explained in this fashion which still leaves the thorny problem of "what adaptive circumstances, evolutionary processes, induced the migration" unanswered (Binford, 1962: 218). A second approach is the proselytizing priests, so much in vogue, particularly in New World archaeology. Interestingly, this explanation has been little favored in the Near East.

A model of interregional trade may be used to shed some light on these two problems. Downs and Ekvall's (1965: 169) paper on Tibet[2] asked a similar question: In Tibet what mechanism is responsible for the "remarkable cultural, linguistic, and social homogeneity within an area in which one would expect a high degree of diversity and socio-political separation?" Their answer is that the entire region is "bound together by a network of trade ..." (p. 182). Long distance trade in Tibet may be initiated by either village cooperatives or by monasteries. Trade and religion crosscut all segments of Tibetan society. The result is a steady stream of goods, persons, and ideas to all parts of the country.

As Hole and Flannery (1968: 196) point out, by 4000 B.C. there are similarities in stylistic attributes of Ubaidian affinity which stretch from Syria, Palestine, and southern Mesopotamia to the Turkoman steppe (cf. Lines, n.d.). Within this area are numerous regional variants (e.g., the Bayat phase in the Deh Luran). The number of these regional variants is still not known, but they appear to relate to single valleys or valley systems and may be considered as ethnic or tribal entities.

As in Tibet or Swat, Pakistan (Barth, 1956), each of these valley systems seems to represent one local economic sphere, much the same as, for example, the contemporary Kirman Basin situation described by English (1966). Tribal affinity and the movement of local foodstuffs within each valley system may be contrasted with the exchange of raw materials and finished craft items into adjacent and more distant valley or economic systems. These latter goods were designated for and utilized primarily by higher status individuals and lineages.

This latter point calls to mind a model recently proposed by Flannery (1968b) to deal with "Olmec influence" during the Formative Period in the Valley of Oaxaca, Mexico. There are a number of similarities in the two cases: (1) both involve emerging elites expressing their differential status through ornaments of exotic raw materials; (2) they show interregional exchange of raw materials and exotic craft items; (3) there is evidence of the spread of religious and stylistic motifs; (4) and evidence of village or full-time craft specialization on the sites.

Flannery's model, based on ethnographic analogies, predicts that the interregional flow of goods should link the highest ranking lineages of the groups involved (cf. Leach, 1954, for the jade trade in Highland Burma). It also predicts that while local subsistence

---

[2] The similarities between the Tibetan and Near Eastern situations were first pointed out to me by K. V. Flannery.

will probably remain unchanged, religion, stylistic motifs, and various forms of symbolism will pass from one area to a high ranking lineage in another, "insofar as it would enhance their own status among their own people." The third prediction is that the areas which form exchange systems will be the most highly developed and not the least developed. A final prediction is that the exotic goods will tend to be taken out of circulation (e.g., in burials). Thus, new goods will have to be acquired, hence maintaining the system.

These conditions appear to be met in Mesopotamia. The products of this long distance trade are recovered in apparently high status burials or in single houses. The major area showing this influence from the southern Ubaid is northern Mesopotamia. During the southern Ubaid 2, the stylistic complex of northern Mesopotamia was totally unlike that to the south, and is called Halafian. At this time, however, it was one of the most highly developed areas in the Near East, as may be seen from the archaeological remains at Tepe Gawra, Nineveh, Arpachiyah, Chagar Bazar, and the Balikh Valley sites. Further, there is no evidence to suggest there was a fundamental change in subsistence patterns accompanying the displacement of the Halafian by the spread of Ubaid stylistic elements into the area.

Most of the areas participating in the use of Ubaid stylistic symbols had been in some way connected prior to this time through the exchange of raw materials. This may be seen through the obsidian trade as outlined earlier.

It would now be useful to have more concrete date for many problems. (1) How far and in what quantity were goods from specialty sites like Murian and Tal-i-Iblis being traded? (2) What evidence is there for Ubaid influence in Badakhshan, the region which holds the source of lapis lazuli and other raw materials? It was on the historic trade routes, but is almost entirely unknown for the prehistoric period. (3) In what quantity are nonlocal goods appearing on each of the five settlement types suggested for this time period? In each case, then, a program of analysis should be initiated to discover the source of the raw materials in the same manner as that used for the obsidian.

Data from these types of questions could then be utilized to test other hypotheses. For example, given the concentration of exotic goods in situations of high status, would expect them to occur only rarely in three of our settlement types: small irrigation farming villages lacking temples, pastoral camps, or permanent villages oriented toward dry farming. Metal, for example, is absent at Ras Al'Amiya (Stronach, 1961). During the Early Dynastic, the pattern discussed here is much clearer. Significantly, from the excavations of the Early Dynastic rural village of Sakheri Sughir (c. 2800 B.C.) in southern Mesopotamia, there was one piece of metal (from the surface) and only two carnelian beads (H. T. Wright, in press).

The Downs and Ekvall and Flannery models of interregional trade are not mutually exclusive. In fact, they are complementary in that they each deal with separate phases of the same problem. They are both hypotheses, and, as such, will need further testing, then possibly refinement and revision. With this, we may end this section by paraphrasing a recent statement of Flannery's (1968 b: 108) which conveniently summarizes the theme presented here. The spread of Ubaid stylistic attributes was not the primary cause of the unity expressed by the archaeological remains, but is only "one reflection of the fact that it was already united in an economic sense."

Finally, we may conclude that the "self-sufficient peasant village" which many investigators like to attribute to the Neolithic and Chalcolithic Near East never existed. The last nearly self-sufficient people were probably hunters and gatherers. With the permanent settlement of a single ecological zone, the products of other zones could not be directly exploited. The data presented by Flannery (1968 a), however, demonstrate that the same food products were being utilized by Neolithic farmers as by Late and post-Pleistocene hunters and gatherers in Iran. The argument here is that by the Late Ubaid each of the settlement types was dependent to some degree upon food exchanges, and the long distance trade of raw materials was a separate system, involving only the higher status individuals and families.

V
CONCLUSIONS

THE BASIC, underlying question discussed in this work has been prehistoric trade in the Near East. Although trade, and the subsequent contact between prehistoric groups, is often evoked as an explanation for culture change, the mechanics of trade as a cultural process have seldom been considered in detail. Even Clark's (1952: 241-81) intensive study of trade in prehistoric Europe was largely confined to the plotting of the distribution of certain kinds of raw materials and artifacts on maps, rather than a discussion of the mechanics and effects of the exchanges themselves. Renfrew (in press) outlines the problem as follows: Trade's "particular and sometimes crucial importance lies in a dual status; as the indicator for us today that intercultural contact was taking place, and as a prime motive, among prehistoric groups, for such contact."

This paper has been an analysis of prehistoric trade in one particular area: the Near East between 7500 and 3500 B.C. Following a suggestion by Squier and Davis (1848) and Renfrew (in press), the first major task was to demonstrate that certain raw materials recovered in excavations were from nonlocal sources. That is, we had to determine the sources of the foreign materials and, where possible, the quantity of the material that was being exchanged.

There are now an impressive number of scientific techniques which may be applied to the characterization of raw materials in order to determine their sources. Renfrew (in press) has listed most of these techniques and the materials upon which they have been successfully applied. They include petrological thin sectioning, optical spectrography, x-ray fluorescence, x-ray diffraction, neutron activation analysis, beta-ray back-scatter, infra-red absorption, and cathode luminescence. Raw materials which have been examined with varying degrees of success include obsidian, flint, clay, marble, jade, faience, and glass.

Much of this paper was built around the analysis of obsidian, both its utilization for tools and ornaments and its trade. Obsidian was an extensively used and widely traded raw material, not only in the Near East, but also in the Aegean, Southern Europe, Japan, New Zealand and the South Pacific, Alaska, North America,

Mexico, Central America, and South America. Thus, in each of these areas, where the sources of prehistoric artifacts may be identified, we will have added a useful dimension to our understanding of the prehistory of that region.

It has been demonstrated that each obsidian flow may be distinguished by its elemental analysis (Gordus *et al.*, 1968, Wright, n.d.). Thus, the archaeologist has a useful tool for clearly defining the directions in which this one raw material was moving. Therefore, although Mellaart says that Çatal Hüyük lies near an obsidian deposit at Hasan Dağ, there is still no concrete evidence to suggest that a major portion of the site's wealth was due to the control of the Central Anatolian obsidian trade. In fact, it now appears that Çatal Hüyük was importing its obsidian from the sources near Acigöl a distance of about 225 km. to the northeast (Renfrew *et al.*, 1966).

A second example is the appearance of group 4c obsidian from Lake Van in the Levant during the PPNB. Although there are only a few pieces known in the Levant during this time period, and there are far more samples from Central Anatolian sources, their importance lies in a separate direction. It was at this time that the wild race of wheat found in the Jordan Valley was being transferred from its natural habitat zone and "domesticated" wheat began to appear in the Zagros-Taurus arc. During the PPNB "wild" sheep were introduced into the Jordan Valley from the Zagros. The major economic importance of Lake Van obsidian was not in obsidian as a raw material but rather the results of the contact between the prehistoric groups involved. This contact precipitated the exchange of significant new subsistence items. Thus, the obsidian trade in this instance was "an agent in communication;" it had a cultural significance which far exceeded the economic value of the obsidian.

With this in mind it should be obvious that intensive investigations should be conducted on a variety of raw materials. While in the case of lapis lazuli, where there seems to be but one source area, items like copper, iron oxides, alabaster, and marble appear to have a number of possible sources. Analyses of this type become become particularly valuable in the Near East when we reach a point of cultural development where craft specialty sites are apparent. The economic importance of sites like Tal-i-Iblis can not be assessed until it is known how far and in what quantity the local products were being transported. Was, for example, Yanik Tepe a specialty site for the production of alabaster? It lies on or near the most probable trade route between the major northern

CONCLUSIONS

Mesopotamian sites, the turquoise source at Meshed, and the lapis source in Badakshan. Clearly, this type of analysis is warranted.

In the Near East, the utilization of obsidian begins considerably earlier than the time period under consideration here. It is not until about 7500 B.C., however, that obsidian began to move in any quantity or with any regularity beyond the immediate environs of the source areas. By 7000 B.C. it was found as far south as both the Jordan Valley and the Deh Luran. It was used for tools until replaced by metal ones during the phases immediately postdating Ubaid.

There are some interesting and significant differences in the utilization of obsidian among the three subareas. Due to the relative absence of flint sources in Central Anatolia, obsidian was used for all tool types common to this subarea. Particularly notable are the large projectile points, often tanged and shouldered, which were made during the earlier stages of the Neolithic. The points from Çatal Hüyük are probably the best examples. Cores are also quite common on most Central Anatolian sites. Microlithic elements, however, seem to be lacking at most sites in this subarea.

The use of obsidian for projectile points extended into Syro-Cilicia. However, the large tanged points were also fashioned from flint at sites like Mersin. It is unfortunate that better studied collections of lithic industries are not available from Syro-Cilicia. From the few published descriptions from sites like Mersin and in the Amuq sequence, there appears to be basic similarities between the lithic materials of the two subareas despite Bialor's (1962) denials. In the Levant, obsidian was a minor raw material for the most part. In the Jordan Valley, it was used almost entirely for blades and microblades.

In contrast, projectile points of obsidian were a rarity in the Zagros-Taurus arc. Cores, too, almost never occurred. In many of the earlier Neolithic sites (e.g. Jarmo), obsidian was commonly used for microelements, particularly geometrics. Still, blades of obsidian predominated.

The lithic assemblages of the phases beginning with Hassuna are, in general, still poorly described. Yet it is evident that new uses of the material were appearing. Mirrors occurred at Çatal Hüyük and beads of obsidian are known from the sites from Syro-Cilicia across northern Mesopotamia. Vases, seal stamps, pendants, and amulets are other forms that first show up during the Halaf and Ubaid phases. There are new forms that seem to have been generally rare or absent in Central Anatolia in sites postdating Çatal Hüyük.

The form in which obsidian (or most raw materials) occurs is important to understanding its place in the exchange system and the system itself. Prior to the Halaf phase, obsidian was utilized for hunting equipment and general purpose tools (such as scrapers and blades). It appears to have been evenly distributed on most sites; that is, there is no evidence for the accumulation of this one product by certain individuals. By the Halaf phase, and more intensely so during the Ubaid, status items in obsidian and other raw materials are now apparent. Houses or rooms and burials began to have disparate quantities. By this time, accumulation and not redistribution became general. Thus, the form in which the material was utilized suggests a fundamental change in the social structure, one which included increasing status differentiation.

When the investigator attempts to consider these data from the standpoint of functioning systems, he must take into account a number of ethnographic observations. A discussion of the exchange of raw materials often falls into the type of trade which Harding (1967) calls "long distance trade." This type of trade involves the movement of goods, both raw materials and finished craft items (and occasionally foodstuffs), across a series of ethnic boundaries. The trade of obsidian from Lake Van into the Deh Luran is an example of this type of trade.

It is this kind of trade to which most archaeologists address themselves. But this may be the least significant type of trade. There is often a second and separate sphere of more local exchanges operating. This more local exchange, which generally deals with foodstuffs, may be of far greater economic importance to the major portion of the population. This system may involve no more than two ethnic units, or even distant kinsmen within the same ethnic unit. Harding (1967) has adequately described one such system. The exchanges between Huron agriculturalists and Algonquin hunting bands is a second example (Wright, 1967). Examples more pertinent to this report are the exchanges between nomads and villagers in the Near East.

This type of local trade seems to have originated with the settlement of permanent villages. When ecological zones which were formerly exploited seasonally during the band's movements are no longer visited, continued utilization of the resources or food products specific to these zones often depends primarily upon trade. Thus, it is important to know the local subsistence, the settlement types and the settlement pattern, and the ecology in order to understand the local exchanges which were taking place.

CONCLUSIONS

In the Near East, for example, the ecology, settlement patterns, and subsistence data all seem to indicate that nomadism, as an economic speciality, may have been underway by the sixth millennium B.C. If so, this means that a system of local exchanges between villagers and herders had to be in operation. Both are specialists; the villagers and townsmen as agriculturalists and craftsmen, and the nomad in animal products.

One may, then, utilize the various types of archaeological, geochemical, ecological, and ethnographic data to present a picture of Near Eastern trade between 7500 and 3500 B.C. Sporadic trade is seen during the Natufian and Zarzian phases in the form of *Dentalium* shells, but it is not until about 7500 B.C. that a number of products begin to be moved.

Flannery (1965) has outlined the ecology and subsistence of early post-Pleistocene hunters and early settled villagers in the Near East. A significant change occurred when the four major ecological zones were no longer traversed seasonally by the now settled farmers. Yet, midden debris from sites in this time range indicates that the same types and quantities of food products were still being utilized (Flannery, 1968*a*), which suggests that either villagers traded between zones, continued to visit the ecological zones which were formerly on their migration routes in order to hunt or to graze flocks, or made food exchanges with hunters still occupying these zones.

A second major adaptation which took place during the early phases of the Neolithic saw herders from parent villages moving flocks of sheep and goats into the mountain pastures during the summer. This practice seems to be evident by the Bus Mordeh phase in Iran (Hole, 1968). The culmination of this pattern was the economic speciality of nomadism, and a local exchange system involving grains and craft items for animal products presumably accompanied it.

In the Zagros-Taurus arc, there is clear evidence for a long distance trade network by the earliest phases of the Neolithic. The major item being traded was obsidian. One consequence of the long distance trade was the movement of domesticated wheat from the Jordan Valley into the Zagros-Taurus arc and sheep from the latter region into the Levant. The obsidian analyses presented here demonstrate that prehistoric groups in the two subareas were in contact by the PPNB. Even though the quantity of obsidian involved was quite small, the major importance of the obsidian trade was as a vehicle of communication. The new subsistence techniques spread rapidly throughout the entire Near East, probably along the routes already established by the obsidian trade.

During the preceramic Neolithic, Jericho appears to have been one of the largest sites. Anati (1962, 1963) considers Jericho to have been a long distance trading power of some importance, dealing primarily in salt, bitumen, and sulfur as exports, and Central Anatolian obsidian, turquoise, and cowrie shells as the main imports. Anati's interpretation does not take into account the oasis location of Jericho, nor the agricultural and wild grain potential of the immediate environs of the site. It would seem as reasonable to approach Jericho as a regional economic center which connected the small villages in the Jordan Valley (e.g. Munhata) and to the south (e.g. Beidha) into a local trade network, and then tied this network into a series of long distance trade systems extending into the Central Anatolian Plateau and the Zagros-Taurus arc. Only more extensive publication of the material from Jericho and the smaller local sites will provide enough data to solve this problem.

A further problem concerns the turquoise and copper in the Ali Kosh phase in the Deh Luran. Is the turquoise from the region around Meshed, or did it come from the Sinai through Jericho? Jericho is the only contemporary site with turquoise. Also, is the copper from one of the Iranian mines or from Maden mines approximately 20 km. from the site of Çayönü? If it is from the latter, it could easily have followed the obsidian from the Lake Van region into the Deh Luran.

By the end of the preceramic and the early stages of the ceramic phases of the Neolithic, there are enough data to indicate that a number of sites were participating in the obsidian trade. Further, although the quantity remains small, there was continued utilization of copper and turquoise, and the addition of new raw materials like alabaster, greenstone, iron oxides, etc., to the trade network. By the second half of the sixth millennium B.C., it is evident that certain products from the long distance trade were being channeled into single households (e.g. at Tell es-Sawwan).

The current settlement pattern and artifact data suggest a series of fully settled farming villages in the lower elevations of the Zagros Valley systems and herders' encampments in the higher reaches of the same valleys by 5500 B.C. Hole (1968) believes that by this time transhumant nomadism was an important additive to the local economy and that nomads were the vehicle by which many of the products were being exchanged.

By the Halaf and Ubaid phases we are on less firm ground when discussing local subsistence. It is only from the Deh Luran

CONCLUSIONS

that good data are available. It is particularly unfortunate that there are no subsistence data from the large and important sites of Arpachiyah, Chagar Bazar, Nineveh, and Tepe Gawra in northern Mesopotamia and Eridu and Ubaid in southern Mesopotamia. By the Late Ubaid, the major sites in northern Mesopotamia, particularly Tepe Gawra, were participating in an extensive long distance trade network in raw materials which extended 1500 miles to the lapis mines in Afghanistan.

A second feature of this time period was the appearance of villages which seem to have been specializing in a particular raw material or craft item. Sites like Tilki Tepe, Murian, and Tal-i-Iblis seem to have depended largely upon the production of craft items or raw materials for their subsistence. Thus, they were an integral part of the expanding trade network. An analysis of the distribution, forms, production, and trade of copper during this time interval would be worthy of a separate study in itself.

Two interrelated hypotheses were presented here to deal with the extensive long distance trade and spread of Ubaid stylistic elements during Ubaid 3. It was suggested that, following the model designed by Downs and Ekvall (1965), an extensive long distance trade network linking the major towns could have been responsible for the spread of Ubaid. There is no need to call upon large scale migrations of people fashioning Ubaid ceramics from southern alluvial Mesopotamia. There is no evidence of extensive warfare during the Ubaid, and sites like Tepe Gawra would have been capable of producing a sizeable defensive force.

There is, however, abundant evidence of the movement of raw materials. Further, there appears to be an accumulation of these trade goods in situations suggesting increasing status differentiation (e.g. in burial or in single rooms or houses). Flannery (1968*b* has proposed a model of interregional trade which predicts that in a case of this type trade goods will link the high ranking lineages of the groups involved. Second, one group will adopt the symbols of the second group insofar as it will enhance their own status. This model would further account for the rapid spread of Ubaid stylistic elements over this large area. In short, the spread of Ubaid took place across a series of ethnic boundaries, but the people in these groups were undoubtedly already linked economically.

It should be quite clear that the hypotheses presented here are still to be tested. Most of the relevant data, particularly those data which deal with local trade and subsistence, are lacking. From the site reports it appears that the data were never recognized nor collected. The source data for raw materials other than obsidian, and probably lapis lazuli, are also very poor. There is still much work to be accomplished in these fields.

Trade is not a panacea for explaining problems of culture change and the appearance of nonlocal raw materials and craft items on prehistoric sites. To assert that trade occurred answers nothing. One must attempt to demonstrate how the system operated, what its consequences were, and the hypotheses must be testable. There is still much to be learned about prehistoric trade.

REFERENCES

Adams, Robert McM.
    1966 The Evolution of Urban Society: Early Mesopotamia and Prehistoric Mexico. Aldine Publishing Co. Chicago.

Altinli, İ. Enver
    1964 Explanatory Text of the Geological Map of Turkey: Van. Maden Tetkik ve Arama Enstitüsü Vayinlarindan. Ankara.

Anati, Emmanuel
    1962 Prehistoric Trade and the Puzzle of Jericho. Bulletin of the American Schools of Oriental Research, 167: 25-31, Baltimore.

    1963 Palestine Before the Hebrews. Alfred A. Knopf. New York.

Barth, Fredrik
    1956 Ecologic Relationships of Ethnic Groups in Swat, North Pakistan. American Anthropologist, 58: 1079-89. Menasha.

    1964 Nomads of South Persia. Universitetsforlaset. Oslo.

Bar-Yosef, O. and E. Tchernov
    1966 Archaeological Finds and the Fossil Faunas of Natufian and Microlithic Industries at Hayonim Cave (Western Galilee, Israel). Israel Journal of Zoology, 15: 104-40. Jerusalem.

Berndt, Ronald, R.
    1951 Ceremonial Exchange in Western Arnhem Land. Southwestern Journal of Anthropology, 7: 156-76. Albuquerque.

Bialor, Perry A.
    1962 The Chipped Stone Industry of Çatal Hüyük. Anatolian Studies, 22: 67-110. London.

Binford, Lewis R.
    1962 Archaeology as Anthropology. American Antiquity, 28: 217-25. Salt Lake City.

Bordaz, Jacques
    1966 Suberde. Anatolian Studies, 16: 32-33. London.

Braidwood, Linda
    1961 The General Appearance of Obsidian in Southwest Asia and the Microlithic Side-Blow Blade-Flake in Obsidian. *In*: Bericht über den V. Internationalen Kongress für Vor-und Frügeschichte Hamburg 1958: 142-47, Verlag Gebr. Mann. Berlin.

Braidwood, Robert J.
 1960 Seeking the World's First Farmers in Persian Kurdistan. Illustrated London News, 237: 695-97. London.
 1967 Prehistoric Men. Scott, Foresman, and Company. Glenview, Illinois.

Braidwood, Robert J. and Linda Braidwood
 1960 Excavations in the Plain of Antioch, I. Oriental Institute Publications, Vol. 61, University of Chicago Press. Chicago.

Braidwood, Robert J., Linda Braidwood, J. G. Smith, and Charles Leslie
 1952 Matarrah: A Southern Variant of the Hassunan Assemblage, Excavated in 1948. Journal of Near Eastern Studies, 11: 2-75. Chicago.

Braidwood, Robert J. and Bruce Howe
 1960 Prehistoric Investigations in Iraqi Kurdistan. University of Chicago Press. Chicago.

Burney, C. A.
 1962 Excavations at Yanik Tepe, Azerbaijan, 1961: Second Preliminary Report. Iraq, 24: 134-52. London.

 1964 The Excavations at Yanik Tepe, Azerbaijan, 1962: Third Preliminary Report. Iraq, 26: 54-61. London.

Burton-Brown, T.
 1962 Excavations in Shahriyar, Iran. Archaeology, 15: 27-31. New York.

Caldwell, Joseph R. and S. M. Shahmirzadi
 1966 Tal-i-Iblis: The Kerman Range and the Beginnings of Smelting. Illinois State Museum Preliminary Report No. 7. Springfield.

Cann, J. R. and Colin Renfrew
 1964 The Characterization of Obsidian and its Application to the Mediterranean Region. Proceedings of the Prehistoric Society, 30: 111-33. London.

Clark, J. G. D.
 1952 Prehistoric Europe: The Economic Basis. Philosophical Library. New York.

Contenson, Henri de
 1963 New Correlations between Ras Shamra and al' Amuq. Bulletin of the American School of Oriental Research, 172: 35-40. Baltimore.

Cressey, George B.
 1960 Crossroads: Life and Land in Southwest Asia. J. B. Lippincott Co. Chicago.

Dixon, J. E., J. R. Cann, and Colin Renfrew
 1968 Obsidian and the Origins of Trade. Scientific American 218, No. 3: 38-46. New York.

Downs, J. F. and R. B. Ekvall
    1965 Animal and Social Types in the Exploitation of the Tibetan Plateau. *In*: Man, Culture, and Animals, edited by A. Leeds and A. P. Vayda, American Association for the Advancement of Science, Publication 78: 169-84. Washington.

Egami, Namio
    1957 The Excavations at Telul Ath-Thalathat. Sumer, 13: 5-22. Baghdad.

El-Wailly, Faisal and Behnam Abu es-Soof
    1965 The Excavations at Tell es-Sawwan: First Preliminary Report (1964). Sumer, 21: 17-32. Baghdad.

English, P. W.
    1966 City and Village in Iran: Settlement and Economy in the Kirman Basin. University of Wisconsin Press. Madison.

Flannery, Kent. V.
    1965 The Ecology of Early Food Production in Mesopotamia. Science, 147: 1247-55. Washington.

    1968*a* Origins and Ecological Effects of Early Domestication in Iran and the Near East. Presented at the Seminar on "The Domestication and Exploitation of Plants and Animals," May 18-19. London.

    1968*b* The Olmec and the Valley of Oaxaca: A Model for Inter-Regional Interaction in Formative Times. *In*: Dumbarton Oaks Conference on the Olmec, pp. 79-110. Trustees for Harvard University. Washington, D.C.

French, D. H.
    1966 Excavations at Can Hasan, Fifth Preliminary Report. Anatolian Studies, 16: 113-24. London.

Fried, Morton H.
    1967 The Evolution of Political Society: An Essay in Political Anthropology. Random House. New York.

Frison, George, Gary A. Wright, James B. Griffin, and Adon A. Gordus
    1968 Neutron Activation Analysis of Obsidian: An Example of its Relevance to Northwestern Plains Archaeology. Plains Anthropologist, 13: 209-18. Lincoln.

Gadd, C. J.
    1937 Tablets from Chagar Bazar, 1936. Iraq, 4: 178-85. London.

Garstang, John
    1953 Prehistoric Mersin. Clarendon Press. Oxford.

Girshman, R.
    1954 Iran. Pelican Books, Richard Clay and Co., Ltd. Bungay. Suffolk.

Goldman, Hetty
1956 Excavations at Gözlü Kule, Tarsus, II. Princeton University Press. Princeton.

Gordus, Adon A., Gary A. Wright, and James B. Griffin
1968 Obsidian Sources Characterized by Neutron Activation Analysis. Science, 161: 382-84. Washington.

Griffin, James B., Adon A. Gordus, and Gary A. Wright
1969 Identification of the Sources of Hopewellian Obsidian in the Middle West. American Antiquity, 34: 1-14. Salt Lake City.

Haggett, Peter
1965 Locational Analysis in Human Geography. St. Martin's Press. New York.

Harding, Thomas G.
1967 Voyagers of the Vitiaz Strait: A Study of a New Guinea Trade System. University of Washington Press. Seattle.

Harlan, Jack R. and D. Zohary
1966 Distribution of Wild Wheats and Barley. Science, 153: 1074-80. Washington.

Herman, Georgina
1968 Lapis Lazuli: The Early Phases of its Trade. Iraq, 30: 21-57. London.

Hole, Frank
1959 A Reanalysis of Basal Tabbat al-Hamman, Syria. Syria, 36: 149-83. Paris.

1968 Evidence of Social Organization in Western Iran: 8000-4000 B.C. In: New Perspectives in Archaeology, edited by S. and L. Binford: 245-68, Aldine Publishing Co. Chicago.

n.d. Chipped Stone Analysis and the Early Village-Farming Community. Unpublished Doctoral Dissertation, 1961, on file in the Oriental Institute, University of Chicago.

Hole, Frank and Kent V. Flannery
1968 The Prehistory of Southwestern Iran: A Preliminary Report. Proceedings of the Prehistoric Society, 33: 147-206. London.

Hole, Frank, Kent V. Flannery and James A. Neely
1969 Prehistory and Human Ecology of the Deh Luran Plain. An Early Village Sequence from Khuzistan, Iran. Memoirs of The Museum of Anthropology, University of Michigan, No. 1, Ann Arbor.

Iddings, Joseph P.
1899 The Rhyolites. In: The Geology of Yellowstone National Park, Part II. United States Geological Survey Monograph No. 32: 356-432. Washington.

REFERENCES

Kirkbride, D.
    1966 Five Seasons at the Pre-Pottery Neolithic Village of Beidha in Jordan. Palestine Exploration Quarterly, 98: 8-72. London.

Lapparent, A. de, P. Bariand, and J. Blaise
    1965 Une visite au gisement de lapis lazuli de Sar-e-Sang (Hindou Kouch, Afghanistan). Comptes Rendus, Société Geologique de France. Feb. 8: 30. Paris.

Leach, E. R.
    1954 Political Systems of Highland Burma. Beacon Press. Boston.

LeBreton, L.
    1957 The Early Periods at Susa, Mesopotamian Relations. Iraq, 19: 79-124. London.

Lines, Joan
    n.d. The Al 'Ubaid Period in Mesopotamia and its Persian Affinities. Unpublished Doctoral Dissertation, 1953, copy on file at the Oriental Institute, University of Chicago.

Lloyd Seton
    1948 The Oldest City of Sumeria: Establishing the Origins of Eridu. The Illustrated London News, Sept. 11: 303-05. London.

Lloyd, Seton and Fuad Safar
    1945 Tell Hassuna. Journal of Near Eastern Studies, 4: 255-89. Chicago.

Mallowan, M. E. L.
    1936 The Excavations at Tall Chagar Bazar and an Archaeological Survey of the Habur Region, 1934-35. Iraq, 3: 1-59. London.

    1937 The Excavations at Tall Chagar Bazar and an Archaeological Survey of the Habur Region: Second Campaign. Iraq, 4: 91-177. London.

    1946 Excavations in the Balih Valley, 1938. Iraq, 8: 111-59. London.

    1947 Excavations at Brak and Chagar Bazar. Iraq, 9: 1-257. London.

    1965 The Mechanics of Ancient Trade in Western Asia. Iran, 3: 1-8. London.

Mallowan, M. E. L. and J. Cruikshank Rose
    1935 Prehistoric Assyria: The Excavations at Tall Arpachiyah, 1933. Iraq, 2: 1-178. London.

Mellaart, James
    1954 Preliminary Report on a Survey of Pre-Classical Remains in Southern Turkey. Anatolian Studies, 4: 175-240. London.

    1958 The Neolithic Obsidian Industry of Ilicapinar and its Relations. Istanbuler Mitteilungen, 8: 82-92. Istanbul.

1960 Excavations at Hacilar, Third Preliminary Report. Anatolian Studies, 10: 83-104. London.

1964 Excavations at Çatal Hüyük, 1963. Anatolian Studies, 14: 39-119. London.

1965a Catal Hüyük West. Anatolian Studies, 15: 135-56. London.

1965b Earliest Civilizations of the Near East. McGraw-Hill Book Company. New York.

1967 Çatal Hüyük: A Neolithic Town In Anatolia. McGraw-Hill Book Company. New York.

Mortenson, Peder
1964 Additional Remarks on the Chronology of Early Village-Farming Communities in the Zagros Area. Sumer, 20: 28-36. Baghdad.

Mortenson, Peder, J. Meldgaard, and H. Thrane
1964 Excavations at Tepe Guran, Luristan. Acta Archaeologica, 39: 110-21.

Orni, E. and E. Efrat
1964 Geography of Israel. Israel Program for Scientific Translations. Jerusalem.

Perkins, Ann L.
1949 The Comparative Archaeology of Early Mesopotamia. Studies in Ancient Oriental Civilization, No. 25, University of Chicago Press. Chicago.

Perrot, Jean
1951 Le Terrase d'el Khiam. In: Le Paléolithique et Mésolithique du Desert de Judee, edited by R. Neuville, Archives de l'Institute de Paleontologie Humaine, 24: 134-78. Paris.

1967 Munhata, un village préhistorique dan le valle du Jordian. Bible et Terre Sainte, 93: 3-16. Paris.

Pfeiffer, R. H.
1940 The Excavations at Van, 1939. Bulletin of the American School of Oriental Research, 78: 31-32. Baltimore.

Piggott, Stuart
1965 Ancient Europe. Aldine Publishing Co. Chicago.

Price, John A.
1967 Conditions in the Development of Silent Trade. Kroeber Anthropological Society, 36: 67-79. Berkeley.

Renfrew, Colin
1969 The Sources and Supply of Deh Luran Obsidian. In: The Prehistory and Human Ecology of the Deh Luran Plain, by F. Hole, K. Flannery, and J. Neely. Memoirs of The Museum of Anthropology, University of Michigan, No. 1. Ann Arbor.

In Trade and Culture Process in European Prehistory. Current
Press Anthropology. Utrecht.

Renfrew, Colin, J. E. Dixon, and J. R. Cann
    1965 Obsidian in the Aegean. The Annual of the British School at Athens, 60: 225-47. Oxford.

    1966 Obsidian and Early Culture Contact in the Near East. Proceedings of the Prehistoric Society, 32: 30-72. London.

Speiser, E. A.
    1935 Excavations at Tepe Gawra, I. University of Pennsylvania Press. Philadelphia.

Squier, E. G. and E. H. Davis
    1848 Ancient Monuments of the Mississippi Valley. Smithsonian Contributions to Knowledge, Vol. 1. Washington.

Stanner, W. E. H.
    1933 Ceremonial Economics of the Malluk and Madngella Tribes of
    -34 the Daly River, North Australia: A Preliminary Paper. Oceania, 4: 156-75, 458-71. Sydney.

Stekelis, M. and Tamar Yizraely
    1963 Excavations at Nahal Oren—Preliminary Report. Israel Exploration Journal, 13: 1-12. Jerusalem.

Stronach, David
    1961 Excavations at Ras al 'Amiya. Iraq, 23: 95-137. London.

Stuckenrath, R. and E. K. Ralph
    1965 University of Pennsylvania Radiocarbon Dates VIII. Radiocarbon, 7: 187-99. New Haven.

Taylor, J. du Plat, M. V. Seton-Williams, and J. Waechter
    1950 The Excavations at Sakçe Gözü. Iraq, 12: 53-138. London.

Tobler, Arthur J.
    1950 Excavations at Tepe Gawra, II. University of Pennsylvania Press. Philadelphia.

Todd, Ian A.
    1966 Aşikli Hüyük—A Protoneolithic Site in Central Anatolia. Anatolian Studies, 16: 139-64. London.

    1968 The Dating of Aşikli Hüyük in Central Anatolia. The American Journal of Archaeology, 72: 157-58. Princeton, New Jersey.

Todd, Ian A. and Giorgio Pasquare
    1965 The Chipped Stone Industry of Alva Dağ. Anatolian Studies, 15: 95-112. London.

van Loon, Maurits
    1966 First Results of the 1965 Excavations at Tell Mureybat near Meskene. Annales Archaeologiques Arabes Syriennes, 16: 211-17. Damascus.

Watson, Patty Jo
    1965 The Chronology of North Syria and North Mesopotamia from 10,000 B.C. to 2000 B.C. *In*: Chronologies in Old World Archaeology, edited by R. W. Ehrich: 61-100. University of Chicago Press. Chicago.

Wertime, Theodore A.
    1968 A Metallurgical Expedition through the Persian Desert. Science, 159: 927-35. Washington.

Winters, Howard D.
    1968 Value Systems and Trade Cycles of the Late Archaic in the Midwest. *In*: New Perspectives in Archeology, edited by S. and R. Binford: 175-222. Aldine Publishing Company. Chicago.

Woolley, C. Leonard
    1934 The Prehistoric Pottery of Carchemish. Iraq, 1: 146-62. London.

Wright, Gary A.
    1967 Some Aspects of Early and Mid-Seventeenth Century Exchange Networks in the Western Great Lakes. Michigan Archaeologist, 13: 181-97. Ann Arbor.

    n.d. Obsidian Analyses and Early Trade in the Near East: 7500-3500 B.C. Doctoral Dissertation, 1968, the University of Michigan.

Wright, Gary A, and Adon A. Gordus
    In Press *a* Source Areas for Obsidian Recovered at Munhata, Beisamoun, El Khiam, and Hazorea. Israel Exploration Journal. Jerusalem.

    In Press *b* Obsidian Groups in the Zagros-Taurus Arc and Southern Alluvial Mesopotamia. Türk Tarih Kurumu Belleten. Ankara.

    1969 Distribution and Utilization of Obsidian from Lake Van Sources between 7500 and 3500 B.C. American Journal of Archaeology, 70: 75-77. Princeton.

Wright, Gary A., Adon A. Gordus, Peter Benedict, and M. Özdoğan
    In Press Location and Chemical Identification of Some Obsidian Sources in the Nevşehir-Aksaray-Niğde Region, Central Turkey. Türk Tarih Kurumu Belleten. Ankara

Wright, Henry T.
    In Press The Administration of Rural Production in an Early Mesopotamian Town. Anthropological Papers, Museum of Anthropology, University of Michigan. Ann Arbor.

www.ingramcontent.com/pod-product-compliance
Lightning Source LLC
LaVergne TN
LVHW021232180326
833917LV00012B/392